NORA HARTQUIST & PATTI LERCH

RETIRE Plugged In

The Ultimate Guide to All Your Retirement Questions

Everything You Need to Know About Social Security, Medicare, Long-Term Care, IRAs, Estate Planning, Incapacity Planning, and More!

BEST SELLER PUBLISHING

Published by Best Seller Publishing®, St. Augustine, FL
Best Seller Publishing® is a registered trademark.
Printed in the United States of America.
ISBN: 978-1-959840-49-7

For more information, please write:

Best Seller Publishing®
53 Marine Street
St. Augustine, FL 32084
or call 1 (626) 765-9750

Visit us online at:
www.BestSellerPublishing.org

The material provided in this book contains general information to help you understand basic tax and retirement planning strategies and considerations. Nothing in this book should be construed as a recommendation to buy or sell any financial vehicle, nor should it be used to make decisions today about your investments, taxes, or retirement planning.

The goal of this book is to expose you to ideas and financial vehicles that may help you work toward your financial goals. Please understand that we cannot make any promises or guarantees that you will accomplish such goals. Investing involves risk, including the potential loss of principal. Past performance is no guarantee of future results.

Neither this book nor its authors may give tax or legal advice. You are encouraged to consult with a qualified professional such as a CPA, enrolled agent, or attorney before making any purchasing decisions.

Despite efforts to be accurate and current, this presentation may contain out-of-date information; we are under no obligation to advise you of any changes related to the topics discussed in this book post-publication.

The authors are in no way employed by, affiliated with, or endorsed by the Internal Revenue Service (IRS), the Social Security Administration, or any other governmental agency.

All examples are hypothetical and for illustrative purposes only.

Actual results will vary. No part of this book is intended to make an offer of sale or purchase of any specific security or insurance product.

TABLE OF CONTENTS

INTRODUCTION

We called this book *Retire Plugged In* so you can "plug in" to all the answers you need. Thesaurus.com says other words for "plugged in" are brilliant, conversant, discerning, experienced, informed, smart, learned, well-informed . . . and we're sure you want to be *all* of that in retirement! Retirement has become so complex most retirees don't even know all the decisions they have to make. As a result, they stress, search, worry, and make mistakes that can ruin their "golden years." We want to plug your retirement in to the answers you need, when you need them, so you can stop worrying, unplug yourself, and enjoy a successful retirement! Most people are all too aware that one decision-making mistake can wreck their future. Our goal is not just to get you TO retirement but also THROUGH retirement, free from the worry of making a mistake DURING retirement! We don't want you to worry about choosing the wrong investment, or not understanding an important government rule about Individual Retirement Accounts (IRAs), Medicare, Social Security, taxes, or estate planning. We don't want you to miss a change in one of these rules that could damage your future.

As you approach retirement, you may not know what you're looking for, let alone the right questions to ask. If you have questions, you may not know where to go to get the answers. When you do find answers, how do you know if they're accurate? What do you do if the information simply doesn't make sense to you?

You may think, "I have enough money, but how do I make sure it lasts as long as I do?" You may be worrying about whether you've adequately prepared. Maybe you're confused by all the conflicting information out there. National radio advertisements insist that annuities are the answer. The next week it could be investments. The week after it could be life insurance. So, which is it?

Insurance companies may insist that they are financial planners, while their ultimate goal is often to push a product. You may hear things about senior scams. And you might see celebrities like Tom Selleck or Henry Winkler on a commercial, offering a small piece of what could be the pie. What they're selling might be the answer for you. Or it might not be.

Maybe you're wondering what might happen if you lose your spouse. What happens if you or your spouse becomes incapacitated? What if you and your spouse *both* become incapacitated? How do you handle your finances then? And if you retire at the age of 65, and you're married, statistics show that one of you may make it to 95. That's 30 years that your assets have to last! You'll need to plan for that.

Should you downsize your home? Should you move closer to your kids? Who's going to help you figure all this out? How can you find these answers?

You may worry about trusting the information you find on websites. Is it up to date? Reliable? And how do you know that other people you talk to are giving you the proper advice? They have been hearing things through the grapevine too. They've had their own experiences and can probably tell you about a family member who did this or that with certain results. But will these experiences match up with your situation? How can you know?

You may be confused by unfamiliar and ambiguous industry terms. Rollovers. Transfers. IRAs. Roths. RMDs. What is a reverse mortgage? Will it work for me? How do I maximize Social Security? Am I even eligible?

And there are all kinds of rules! State rules. Federal rules. What can you do? What can't you do? "I put money in for 30 years, so now I just take it out, right?" "Oh, I have to pay taxes?" "Oh, there's some rule I have to be aware of to avoid being penalized *50%?"*

Decisions made without proper planning can be life threatening. This is why we, Nora and Patti, wrote this book, *Retire Plugged In*—so that you're plugged in to the answers to the nine retirement decisions you must not "blow," as explained in Chapters 1–9. Everything in this book has been garnered from our collaboration working with clients. We have helped hundreds of people ready to make the biggest decisions they will ever make on the largest asset they have, with no idea if they have the right information. We have all heard, "Experience is the best teacher." Let our experience avoid bad experiences for you. We want to plug you in to the answers you need.

We both entered financial planning because we made the mistake of listening to advisors who did not have our best interests at heart. Patti's husband lost 100% of his retirement after listening to an "advisor" who sold him something he didn't understand. Similarly, Nora and her ex-husband bought several financial products thinking they would provide money for college for their children and retirement for them both. Instead, they were devastated to find out several hundred thousand dollars was just *gone*!

We both set out to educate ourselves after these experiences, and we now hold licenses in both investments and insurance. Nora is a member of the Ed Slott Master Elite IRA Advisory Group, the nation's most exclusive group of advisors for expertise in retirement distribution planning. Patti has also been trained by Ed Slott, who has been called "The Best" source for IRA advice by *The Wall Street Journal.* Nora and Patti are both also Certified Estate Planners (CEPs®) and Certified Financial Fiduciaries (CFFs®). As CFFs®, we are required by law to put our clients first, unlike what happened to us! A CFF® must meet rigorous requirements, background checks, pass an exam, and keep up with the latest rules and laws about being a fiduciary. We both also have Certification in Long-Term Care (CLTC®).

Unlike retirement books that focus on a single issue—such as "investing," "income planning," "being happy in retirement," "health issues in retirement," or "traveling in retirement"—this book will help you understand the main concepts essential to *complete* retirement planning. This is because trying to solve an issue without looking at the entire picture may be the biggest mistake you'll ever make! Addressing one issue in isolation often creates another issue you are not prepared for.

This book will introduce you to important retirement issues like long-term care planning, tax planning, and basic Internal Revenue Service (IRS) rules, as well as estate planning, the financial basics of decumulation versus accumulation, and the importance of planning ahead and following through. As you read the chapters, it may be a revelation to you how outrageous and complicated the rules of retirement can be—from Medicare to Social Security, Medicaid, pension options, investing, creating income, RMDs, and even taxation. These concepts will be presented through case studies from clients we have worked with, based on actual experiences they have had. After reading this book, you will be aware of the most common pitfalls to avoid.

This book includes our overall retirement solution, which requires allocating your money into three pots. To put these three pots together for our clients, we do something called a Life Income–Living Asset Cycle℠. In this assessment, we explain how you can figure out how to allocate your funds. You don't have to be a financial wizard to do this. It just means putting all the pieces together so that you have a lifetime income. In this way, we can help you figure out how to cycle through your assets so you have an income that will never run out.

It comforts us to know that hundreds of others are secure because we are here to help. We've written this book and created our membership website to help all the families we couldn't reach otherwise. For those who want to go a bit deeper into retirement planning after reading the book, we offer additional planning tools on our www.RetirePluggedIn.com membership site. With a membership, you can develop your own retirement plan using our proprietary Life Income–Living Asset Cycle℠ method. We'll plug you in to the answers, even when they're continually changing the rules.

Throughout this book we have included links to free resources available only to you because you have invested in your future by purchasing and reading this book. These resources will be updated as rules change, so you can always refer back to them. You're plugged in to all the updates you'll need. Especially for those who feel you can "do it yourself" after reading this book, we urge you to become a member of our site. The website provides the support you need to remain independent. But you will find it helpful while consulting an advisor as well.

Our philosophy is that retirement is a journey not a destination. Think of it like climbing Mount Everest. Without a guide to translate the lingo and help prepare you for the obstacles along your way, you could be risking the rest of your life. Through this book, we want to introduce those on the cusp of retirement to the key terms they need to know and common pitfalls they may encounter so that they can adequately plan.

After reading this book, you will understand the language you need in order to ask the right questions that pertain to your situation. This will enable you to make better decisions. But know that retirement planning is quite complex. For this reason, this book will educate you on how to find an advisor. For many, the right advisor can offer peace of mind. You can rest assured knowing your family is covered and your legacy will be left to those you want to have it.

Whether you choose to do it yourself or seek an advisor, this book aims to show you that retirement planning is very comprehensive. It is not a one-and-done scenario. Everyone is different. Everyone's situation is different. Their families are different. Their goals are different. Their lifestyles are different.

No book can give you a definitive answer as to what you, personally, should do. This book provides information, not advice. We will raise questions you need to consider and give information on the ever-changing, complicated retirement rules you'll encounter with some possible solutions to common problems. But you need to answer each of the questions for yourself to even begin to plan the meaningful, successful retirement that you have worked so hard to enjoy.

Now, let us get started. Let's get an overview of some common retirement myths.

OVERVIEW

Ten Dangerous Retirement Myths

We all look forward to the stage in our life that we call retirement. We imagine ourselves able to do what we want to do when we want to do it. Unfortunately, we only get one chance at getting it right. And if we mess it up, there are no do-overs. It's over.

Take Ed's story as an example. Ed had worked for the federal government for 40 years. When Ed submitted his retirement paperwork, he learned it would cost him 10% of his retirement income to take a survivor benefit for his wife, Elaine. In other words, Ed would have to give up 10% of his retirement income, reducing his pension from $7,000/month to $6,300/month, to guarantee his wife, Elaine, would receive 55% of his pension if he predeceased her. Elaine was on tube feeding due to a condition she'd had for years, so Ed thought she'd probably predecease him. He didn't want to give up $700/month (10%) of his income to guarantee $3,850/month (55%) of his $7,000/month pension for Elaine because she'd probably be gone before him.

But Elaine's feeding tube didn't actually slow her down. She put it in a port by her collarbone nightly, took it out in the morning, and lived her life pretty normally otherwise. She drove, shopped, cleaned house, gardened, and even cooked for Ed.

An "advisor" sold Ed a ten-year term policy for $200,000 since, if Elaine did survive him, it wouldn't be for long. What Ed didn't know was that if Elaine *did* predecease him, he would have had his retirement benefit jump back up from $6,300/month to the full amount, $7,000/month, because he'd no longer need to pay for a survivor benefit. His advisor had not told him that. Unfortunately, Ed got cancer nine years after he retired, and the term insurance would expire with no benefit for Elaine in just one year.

When Ed finally came to us, we put together a Life Income–Living Asset Cycle[SM] plan for income from the $200,000. It wouldn't be enough for Elaine to live as comfortably as she would like, but she'd be able to stay in their home—*if* Ed passed before the policy expired.

If you don't understand the dangers involved, you can blow up your retirement or your spouse's retirement unintentionally. Having helped hundreds of people transition into retirement and *through* retirement, we've learned that incomplete knowledge is only part of the problem. There are also dangerous ideas out there on the internet, in magazines, and in books. Any good retirement planning should take into account these common myths and the pitfalls that can result from believing them.

In this book, we will be defining financial and other terms and explaining their significance. We've also included a glossary in the back of the book.

MYTH #1—RETIREMENT IS A DESTINATION

"All I need is a magic dollar amount, and I have arrived at retirement!"

That's a common misconception. You could have a million dollars, but retirement is not a destination. To use a Mount Everest analogy again, if you have a million dollars, you've done a great job of getting to base camp. Now, you're ready to start the climb.

But there are pitfalls along the way, like inflation, long-term care, and market decline. You have to prepare for these obstacles. This is why it's more helpful to think of retirement as the beginning of a journey. And if you don't look at it that way, then you may not be paying attention to the things you need to. You could wind up falling off a cliff. You might not be able to remain in retirement or be comfortable or happy throughout.

MYTH #2—MY INCOME WILL VIRTUALLY PLAN ITSELF

You might say, "Income planning is simple. I mean, I get Social Security. I even have a pension. Income planning is just about budgeting the money that comes in. I can wait until retirement to do that."

The problem with such an approach is that it doesn't take into account how much income you actually need. Is your house paid off? Are your credit cards paid off? And what about that student loan you cosigned for your granddaughter? And, oh, your mom is looking at assisted living, and you might have to pay for that too.

How are you going to produce income to do all this? Maybe you've got some rental houses, but how do you plan to make money out of those properties? Is it better to sell them? Maybe you have stocks with dividends you can live off of, or even an Individual Retirement Account (IRA). But have you taken into account things like taxes?

The Myth of the IRA

You might also say, "Well, I have this wonderful IRA I rolled over from my 401(k). It's very simple. I'm going to roll that over and just like I put money in every month, I can take money out every month. I'll be able to live on the money. No problem."

It sounds simple enough. But realize that you haven't yet paid taxes on that money. Therefore, if you have a million dollars in your IRA, and you cash it in, you'll have about $650,000 after taxes, if you're lucky. And did you know that the IRS interprets the congressional rules on IRAs and changes the laws as many as 25–50 times a year? These changes aren't in the newspaper. And they can affect your retirement. You can't adequately plan for retirement without an awareness of these challenges.

The Myth of "Asset Allocation"

"Asset allocation will save me in investments. Because after all, if stocks go up and bonds don't, I'm good. If bonds go up and stocks go down, I'm good."

Asset allocation means dividing your money, often between stocks and bonds. Yet this is also a big myth. This strategy may work out for you, if you happen to be in the right place at the right time. What do we mean by that? Well, if you have your money in an investment when the market declines, do you need to take that money out to live on? Will you have enough left that your investments can grow back? If you have to liquidate too many shares, recovery may not be possible.

And what about certificates of deposit (CDs)? Do they keep up with inflation? Will that be a problem? Could you lose the value of the money by putting it in something too safe? Should you try to find something that is safe but grows?

Maybe you've heard the market average is between 6% and 8%. But during the "Lost Decade" of 2000 to 2010, the market was flat. It was zero. The new norm is 3%. If you have a million dollars and can only take out 3%, that's $30,000 a year. Can you live on that? If not, how many millions do you need to live like you're living now? You may need to reconsider how best to invest.

Annuities and Guarantees

"Investments can be scary. I want guarantees. I want to feel safe. I've heard it's really bad if I get into the wrong annuity. I've also heard annuities are a rip-off. They're a scam perpetrated on retirees. I don't want that to happen to me! A well-known high-profile financial advisor is all over TV and magazines, screaming, 'Don't get annuities for your retirement fund!' But is he right? What should I do?"

It depends. If you need guaranteed income you can't outlive, only an insurance company will guarantee that. The husband of one woman we worked with lost all of his retirement. He put it in the stock market and was taking money out to live. Then the market tanked. She came to us and said she wanted guarantees on her retirement money. And so, a portion of her money was put into annuities that guaranteed an income.

The right kind of annuity doesn't have high fees and can't lose money in the market. But there are quite a few different types to know about—fixed, fixed deferred, variable, fixed indexed, single premium, immediate annuities, and CD-type annuities. A retirement planner can direct you toward which one is best for you. You can find video explanations of all types of annuities on the RetirePluggedIn.com membership site.

With a clear plan, you can put all of this together and make sure you've accounted for the money coming in and the money going out. Every tool in this box—the investments, pensions, insurance, the annuities, and even the Social Security—has pros and cons. The key is to learn what's good and bad for you. The tool for you may not be the tool for your neighbor.

MYTH #3—COLLECTING SOCIAL SECURITY IS EASY

"When I'm ready to collect Social Security, all I have to do is go to the Social Security office. They'll tell me everything I need to know there."

Unfortunately, a Social Security employee is not going to sit down and explain the 200+ strategies for collecting Social Security. It is not part of their job to explain the convoluted retirement rules Social Security put into place. However, a financial advisor who specializes in Social Security rules will know that, as of 2015, there are separate rules for three different age groups. This advisor can explain these collection strategies. Or, if you are a RetirePluggedIn.com member, you'll learn about the most beneficial strategies.

A financial advisor can advise you to take Social Security early, or to wait, based on your entire financial picture. An advisor can warn you of traps, for example, if you take Social Security early, you can't go back to work if you need to. In fact, if you make over a certain amount, the Social Security Administration might actually take money back! Accessing your benefits early may even cause you to lose 8% a year for every year below full retirement age. You'll learn more about the ins and outs of Social Security in Chapter 3.

MYTH #4—MY TAXES WILL BE LOWER IN RETIREMENT

"I have my income sorted out, and I think I know how I'm going to live on the money. Taxes are always lower in retirement, so there's no need to worry. And it's not like I can *avoid* taxes. So, what's the use of planning?"

Your taxes will only be lower in retirement *if your income is lower.* So, if your goal is to have less money to spend in retirement, then yes, taxes will be lower. The fact is that most people need to plan for a minimum of 95% of the income they were earning before. Why? Well, now that you're no longer working, you won't have to pay FICA (payroll tax: 7.65% for Social Security, Medicare, and unemployment tax), and you won't be contributing the 10% you were contributing (hopefully!) to your retirement account.

Those retirement account contributions *lowered* your taxes when you were working, but that deduction will go away when you're not working and contributing. Taxes will need to be paid from your IRA, your pension, and your Social Security. Yes, your Social Security too! But with a plan, you can minimize those taxes if you know how to navigate the complicated "provisional income" rules. In Chapter 8, you can find out how.

MYTH #5—ONE CAN LIVE ON HALF THE MONEY OF TWO

"If my spouse passes away, I can keep going on half the money."

It is a myth that one person can live just as well on half the money of two people. Especially if the deceased spouse is the one with the pension, or the larger Social Security check. Does the utility company say, "Hey, pay half the bill on your air conditioning"? Does the state say, "Since he passed away, you don't have to pay real estate taxes"? Of course not.

Pension and Social Security

If there's one of you, you collect one Social Security check. The good news is that you lose the *lower* check. You get to keep the larger one, even if it was your spouse's. But that pension? If it belongs to your deceased spouse, and he or she didn't take a survivor benefit, you get zero!

Oh, but your spouse did take the benefit? Great! Still, the maximum survivor benefit available for most pensions is 50%. So now you only have half the pension coming in. Well, you can cut back some, no problem. Or you can take a little extra out of the IRA. But when you take more out of your IRA, you'll find you're now taxed at a higher rate than when your spouse was alive. What? You need to plan for another absurd retirement rule!

Taxes

There is something we call the "widow's or widower's penalty" imposed by the government. You see, the year after one spouse passes away, the government says, "Ha! You can't file joint anymore. You're not married! You have to file 'single.'"

When you filed joint in 2021, you paid only 12% taxes until your income exceeded $105,050/year (or $80,250 + $24,800 automatic deductions). If you still need that $105,050 to live on when your spouse passes, your taxes go up to 22% when you're single and your income exceeds $53,075 (or $40,525 + $12,550 automatic deduction). When your income exceeds $98,925 (or $86,375 + $12,550), you're taxed at 24% on the same $105,050 income you paid 12% on before your spouse passed!

So right when you need the money the most, your taxes jump from 12% to 24%, or double! Okay, so you'll just take more money out of your IRA. But this can increase taxes on your Social Security. How do you get out of this hole?

Make a Tax Plan

The only way to get out of this hole is to avoid it in the first place. You need to have a plan. In advance. Often, when there is a plan, the first one to go is the one who understood it. Now the survivor is just too upset, and financial devastation soon follows.

Make a plan while you can talk about it. While you can discuss it. While you can both understand it. And then, if something happens, you may be emotionally distraught, but at least you'll be financially stable. We'll talk more about survivorship in Chapter 7 of this book.

MYTH #6—I WON'T HAVE TO WORRY ABOUT MY HEALTH

"I won't have to worry about health problems once I'm retired. I'll have medical insurance or Medicare. Besides that, I take really good care of myself. I'm not like my parents. I don't smoke. I don't eat fried food. I exercise."

Great, so, if you have a heart attack, you're less likely to die. And, if you don't die, you live. When you live, you get old. When you get old, you get sick or frail. And when you're sick or frail, you need care. Obviously, the better we take care of ourselves, the longer we will live, the more we may have to plan for issues down the line, possibly even dementia or Alzheimer's.

Long-term care can be expensive, so you need to plan for it. Medicare will *not* pay for it. Statistics show that it's likely either you or your spouse will need care at some point. We'll talk more about long-term care with overall health care in Chapter 4.

MYTH #7—RETIREMENT IS ALL ABOUT ME

"When I retire, I'll have all the time in the world to do what I want."

Really? If you're married, have you worked out who is going to cook, clean, and shop for groceries? It's essential that you discuss even the day-to-day in order to prepare for retirement with each other.

We've seen couples divorce because with both partners now home all day, they simply couldn't stand each other. And remember, two single people cannot live as well as one couple.

This is why it's important to work out what you are going to do with your spouse when you retire. Take a few vacations beforehand to ensure your visions of retired life are compatible. We'll look at this issue in more detail in Chapter 1.

MYTH #8—STICK WITH YOUR FINANCIAL ADVISOR

"I have done well accumulating money. My advisor has been awesome in helping me do this, so I'm going to stay with this advisor for the rest of my life."

If your advisor did a wonderful job getting you to where you are, that means they're an accumulation specialist. They really know how to accumulate money. That's exactly what you needed when you were *preparing* for retirement.

But now, you want to use this money to live on. You need a decumulation specialist. A decumulation specialist understands all the ins and outs of Social Security, as well as IRA withdrawals and RMDs. And you need someone who can help you create a plan for taxes. We'll go into more detail in Chapter 8 about decumulation and taxes.

Beware the Big, Proprietary Firm

If your current financial advisor works at a big proprietary firm, he is going to give you the "party line." An advisor at these types of firms will push you to do what makes the firm money—not what is in your best interest.

As an example of this, we recently had a prospective client come in. He had a friend who went to work for a large firm and talked him into investing a large part of his retirement money. He came to us when the firm was about to roll his retirement savings over into a product that would lock up his money right when he needed liquidity in retirement.

The product had a 10% penalty if he withdrew too much money (according to their rules). If he left the money to grow, the annual fees were almost 4%. If those fees were withdrawn every year, how much *more* growth would he need to keep up, much less live on it himself? Do you think his friend wanted to hurt him? Of course not. But they bought the party line.

This is why your advisor should not work at a large firm that has its own proprietary products. Your advisor also should not work at a bank. You need someone who is experienced and independent. At one time, Nora worked for a big firm. She left so she could start over and become independent because she wanted to be able to do what was right for clients.

Licensure

Your retirement advisor *should* be licensed in insurance *and* investments. Your advisor should also be a fiduciary. This is particularly important. A fiduciary is someone who, by their license, is required to do what's in your best interest. Not all licenses in investments have fiduciary requirements. Some are just required to do what might be suitable, even if it's in *the advisor's* best interest. Even better, seek out a Certified Financial Fiduciary (CFF®). This is someone who has taken a course and certification test to understand what a true fiduciary should do.

We will discuss how to find an advisor in the final chapter of this book.

MYTH #9—THE MAGIC BULLET

"This all sounds pretty complicated. There must be some magic bullet nobody's telling me about." We hear this all the time. "I just need to keep it simple. Find me that one, safe place, with some growth and put all my money there."

The short answer is that there is no magic bullet. There is no one answer. It depends on your situation and what you're trying to accomplish. It depends on your debts. It depends on what you want. If you have someone you need to support once you're gone, you have to work this out.

These are the two phrases our clients hear the most from us about planning:

1. Keep your options open! (Life is not static. What if your plan needs to change?)
2. It depends! (The best tools and plan depend on *your* situation. Everyone's situation is different!)

MYTH #10—RETIREMENT PLANNING IS SIMPLE

"Retirement planning is simple! I can wait until I'm old enough to retire to start thinking about it. I mean, how hard can it be? I put money in, and then I take money out to live on."

Well, let's back up the truck, because all of the other myths we've discussed contribute to this big one. You're going to have money put away, so you will have some income. Yet even with a pension, there are options to navigate. Do you take a lump sum? Do you take a survivor benefit, or do you pass on it like Ed did?

In the end, Ed passed away a month before the policy ran out. The night he died, his son called us and put the phone by Ed's ear. We assured him we had a plan to keep Elaine in her home. But living on the $200,000 was a struggle for Elaine. She had to give up some of her usual activities because she could no longer afford them. Paying for health care was also a challenge. But she was able to stay in the house until she passed.

So, like Ed, how do you know if you're making the right decisions?

You can't finance retirement like you can finance a house or a college education. You have to plan ahead. And if you live to 95, what will things cost then? Thirty years ago, gasoline went for 25 cents a gallon. And now it's over four dollars! And these are just the basic questions to contemplate. Beyond that, consider the following:

- Do you know how to maximize your Social Security?
- Have you planned for taxes?
- Have you considered other expenses, like updating your home?

- Will Medicare take care of your health care? What about other health insurance? How does Medicaid work? Do you need a long-term care plan?
- Are your retirement plans compatible with your spouse's? Do you want to stay in your home but he wants to move? Does he want to travel but you hate traveling?
- Is your financial advisor the right one for you?

These are the types of questions the myths outlined in this overview likely raised for you. Maybe you've even heard of estate planning and wonder about documents like Powers of Attorney and if you need them. We will get to all of this in the book.

Don't believe anyone who says they have *the* answer. Run for your life! Something that works for your neighbor may be disastrous for your family. If your neighbors have pensions and Social Security, maybe they can risk some of their money in the market. But maybe you shouldn't. You need different strategies for immediate income, future income, and spousal support income. To meet your needs, you will need to look at investments, annuities, Social Security, pensions, and tax-efficient planning—all of which we will cover in upcoming chapters.

You have to consider all of these things in order to come up with a retirement plan that will work *throughout* your retirement. And if it's too overwhelming to look at all this yourself and to research all those complicated retirement rules, then you need to find a qualified advisor to help you.

The first chapter will help you start preparing.

1

PLANNING

Retirement Is *Not* a Destination

Retirement is the beginning of a new journey, the ultimate vacation. **Decision #1: How will I fund my needs after the day I retire?** When we prepare for even a week-long trip, most of us don't just save money and say, "Okay. We're going on vacation." We plan where we want to go, how we're going to get there, and how much money we need for travel, hotels, souvenirs, and activities.

We plan what we are going to do and how we're going to avoid any problems, such as making sure nobody robs us. We make a comprehensive plan. It might take us months to plan for this one week. So, shouldn't we plan even more substantially for 20 to 30 years of, essentially, vacation?

Some people think they can just retire once their bank account reaches a certain amount. James is an example of this. He came to us the week after he retired and said that he had a million dollars. He didn't think he needed a plan. "I just want someone to teach me how to grow my money and keep it safe," he said.

It turns out that James had $170,000 in debt due to his daughter's college education, as well as family problems and emergencies over time.

He thought he'd just take $170,000 out of his million dollars, not realizing he would have to pay 28% to 30% federal taxes on that money, plus 5% in state taxes. Paying off this debt alone would take a quarter of a million dollars out of his retirement money.

What was James to do? Well, the only way we could help him at this point was to make an extraordinarily complex Life Income–Living Asset Cycle℠ plan. James believed that a million dollars was the goal and the end. He hadn't made a solid plan about how he was going to use the money.

MAKE A CHECKLIST!

Many of us find checklists helpful for planning vacations. A checklist can help with retirement planning too.

- ✓ What are we going to take with us?
- ✓ What are we going to do along the way?
- ✓ What will we do if there's an emergency?

Go to www.RetirePluggedIn.com/bookdownloads to create your own checklist for the journey through retirement. You'll learn all about the information your family should gather before retirement.

PLAN ACCORDINGLY

You need to determine what you want to accomplish on this journey into retirement, first of all. Of course, you want to have fun. You want to have free time to be able to do what you want, when you want. But how do you spend time without spending money?

Plan to Enjoy Life

Most of the retirees we've worked with spend 95% of the amount of money they spent when they were working. You might say, "Well, how is that possible? I don't have to commute anymore. I don't have to get nice clothes. I don't have to contribute to my 401(k). I mean, now I'm going to use the money. I don't have to save and contribute. Why would I spend more, or almost the same?"

Well, if you're going to get that RV, or that boat, or buy that vacation place you want to go to every year, then you're going to spend a good deal of money. You're likely going to go out to eat more because you have more time. You're more likely to go out with friends and do things, maybe play golf. All of this costs additional money. You're not just living now. You're enjoying.

Many people ask if they should prepare a budget for retirement. What we recommend is an expense sheet. Expenses are what you *want* to spend and need to plan for, not what you *must* cut yourself down to! This is the difference between a budget and expense sheet.

Plan to Live a Long Time

Many of us were smart enough to not eat a lot of fried foods. Many of us went to the gym and took care of ourselves. What that does, counterintuitively, is give you a problem your parents didn't have . . . a longer life! This means that you'll need more money than your parents did. You have to plan on living a long time and keeping up your lifestyle!

In 1940, five years after the Social Security program was begun, a little over 50% of men ever reached age 65. Those who did were not expected to live more than 12 years beyond that, just into their 70s, according to the Social Security Administration. I (Nora) remember my grandmother. When she was in her 70s, all she did was sit in a rocking chair. She rotated among each of her children's homes so they could take care of her.

But today, according to a TD Ameritrade Women and Aging survey (2018), 73% of women believe 70 is the new 50, and 59% of men agree. These baby boomers are doing as much and more at age 70 than their parents did at age 50. The odds that at least one member of a 65-year-old couple will live to 92 are 50%, and there's a 25% chance at least one of them will reach age 97.[1]

---

1. According to the Society of Actuaries IAM 2000 mortality tables, updated to 2013 with Schedule G Adjustments.

This means that when you retire, you should plan on living into your 90s. If you live on $6,000 a month today at age 65, and inflation averages 3%, which it has for the last 25 years, by the time you're 95, you're going to need over $14,500 a month to live like you do now. This is what makes retirement a long journey, not the destination it resembled so many years ago.

Plan for Death and Frailty

For spouses today who reach age 65, one of them is likely going to survive longer than the other. Even if you own your own home and $100,000 in assets, will that be enough if one of you lives until age 95? So, if you retire at 65, you have to think about funding your retirement for 30 years. You also have to plan what you're going to live on when one of you is alone.

You see, retirement isn't the end of your life. It's the beginning of what we call the third phase of your life. You had childhood. You had your adulthood with your working years. Now you're going into the retirement phase. But that's not the last phase. The industry that we work in has found that there is a fourth phase.

The fourth phase is frailty, because, as we said, if you don't die, you live. If you live, you get old. You get sick. You get frail. Even if we're healthy, our bodies wear out. How do we pay for help if we're frail? How do we account for inflation if we live 30 years? We'll go into this more in following chapters.

CAN YOU COMPROMISE AND BE HAPPY?

Sean and Tina became clients ten years ago. They had no children, and they planned for their retirement far in advance. We put a solid plan together to ensure they would have adequate income for the rest of their lives. The plan even included increases for inflation. They were happy with it, and so were we.

However, when it became time to retire, Sean didn't think he could live with Tina anymore. They did seem ill-suited for each other, but they had been married for 30 years! Sure enough, Sean called us and said sheepishly, "I'm filing for divorce."

What happened to the plan? We'll address that later in this chapter. But the point is this: planning is not about just the money. It's also about knowing how you plan to live once you've retired.

Over 50% of the couples who come to us have divergent ideas of retirement. He wants to downsize. She wants to keep buying stuff. She wants to move south. He doesn't want to. We now spend more time redoing plans because of these problems.

Before retirement comes, a couple has to be in agreement. Where do you both want to live? How do you want to live? How much time do you want to spend together? Can you compromise and both be happy?

Are you going to help the grown children in retirement? This can be a big problem between spouses. Are you going to help the grandchildren? You have to face these decisions together.

FOLLOW-THROUGH IS ESSENTIAL

Mary Ann and Andy came in eleven years ago. We did estate planning and helped them set up a Living Trust, but they never came back to get a checkup on that or to do the financial planning. Andy was a real do-it-yourselfer. He said, "I can follow the instructions on how to do the funding of the Trust. I've got no problem. You gave me the documents. I'm good."

Andy assured us that he had enough pensions and IRAs for both their lives. He didn't need to come in for a checkup. Mary Ann felt out of the loop with what he was doing, but she trusted him to take care of everything.

About four years ago (seven years after they first came in), we got a phone call from Mary Ann. "No matter what happens we've got that Trust, right?" Then she broke down, crying. She said, "Andy has dementia."

Mary Ann couldn't communicate with Andy anymore. He would sometimes even ask their four-year-old grandson to help him to go to the bathroom. We asked Mary Ann if Andy had finished funding the Trust by putting the assets into it.

Mary Ann didn't know. She knew they had money, but she didn't know how much. She didn't know where it was. She didn't know what bills needed to be paid. She came to our office pulling a rolling suitcase full of papers behind her. We found that nothing was in the Trust.

The story of Mary Ann and Andy illustrates why checkups to your retirement plan are not optional. Tweaks need to be made periodically due to life changes. What's the use in starting something if you don't finish it? It can't accomplish its purpose if you don't finish it.

We all pay most attention to the urgent matters in our lives. The water heater broke, and now we must get it replaced. Or the car broke down. Or, let's get those reservations for dinner with our friends. Or, the grandkids are coming over for the weekend. The urgent or immediate is what gets done; the important but less immediate gets ignored. This is why committing to follow through is essential.

We have learned in our practice to set a deadline for checkups. People need to periodically discuss these aspects of their retirement plan *before* disasters occur, not after. Like your doctor's checkups, it's not just time that determines when you need to do a checkup—it's also your particular condition.

FIND YOUR MAGIC NUMBER

How do these stories apply to you? Well, let's start with James's situation. This is the ultimate example of mistaking retirement as a destination. Have you ever asked, "What is my magic number for retirement? Once I have a million dollars, I'm done." If so, you've risked making the same mistake as James.

The financial industry has finally recognized the rate of return safe to withdraw from your retirement savings to be 3%. Of a million dollars, 3% is $30,000. Divide $30,000 by 12 months, and you get $2,500. Can you live on $2,500 a month? And what about inflation? Could more planning be necessary? Absolutely!

James's situation was solved by very complex planning. We had to spread his debt repayment over years because otherwise his Medicare premium would have gone from $170.10/month to $544.30/month.

And his taxes would have gone through the roof! We had to plan for a home equity line of credit and plan how that would be repaid. He then had a medical emergency that was not covered by health insurance, as well as the additional expenses of his grown daughter coming home. This meant even more planning.

James thought he knew his magic number. But you can't know what your magic number is until you plan for your actual situation. Had James just kept pulling money out of his IRA, he would have been broke in less than ten years. Now, James has a complex plan that will provide him money for the rest of his life.

ARE YOUR GOALS COMPATIBLE?

Remember Sean and Tina? Well, they went through with the divorce, even though they had always gotten along fine until then. Their marriage fell apart because they never discussed what they wanted in retirement. Tina wanted to get out of the rat race and spend her time collecting stuff. Sean wanted to live simply, with less clutter. He didn't want her getting upset with him anymore. So, Sean filed for divorce.

Patti and I remained advisors for both of them. We worked out an equitable plan, so that Sean and Tina could both move on financially. Of course, they could not move on *as* comfortably. Tina remained retired, but Sean worked for an additional five years. The lawyers told them we saved them $50,000 in legal fees by negotiating an amicable settlement so they could avoid a court battle. They saved this, at least.

The moral of Sean and Tina's story is very important. If you're married, start discussing the lifestyle you envision in retirement. Will you move, downsize, do volunteer work? Will one of you retire and the other go to a job that you like more? Will you travel? Can you afford it? How badly do you both want that beach house? See if you can work out compromises for the things you don't agree about completely.

Patti and I have worked with at least three couples who were married 40 years without any problems but who decided to divorce. If you plan to stay together, you need to plan for your differences and how you can give each other space. Maybe you've tolerated each other for years because you don't see each other all the time. So, how can you make your relationship work in retirement? Finding compromise beforehand is important.

One couple we worked with never fought. But then she wanted to move north, and he didn't want to. So, she filed for divorce. It's going to devastate both of their finances. And meanwhile, they're still living together and happy. They still go out to eat together. And with another couple we know, he's still cutting her lawn and fixing things at the house but they're divorced. This is why it's important to talk about how we want to live, well before we retire.

ONLY YOU CAN FOLLOW THROUGH

Finally, we've come back to Mary Ann and Andy. Mary Ann's situation is not uncommon. Seldom do both members of a couple know about their finances because one spouse takes that job over. The other one has no idea.

Fortunately for Mary Ann, she and Andy had at least started their planning with us, so she had someone to come to for help. Mary Ann and Andy's situation can be completely avoided if you choose a financial planner who will assist you in following through on your planning, *and* you are willing to do it.

The financial planner should schedule checkups on what you're doing. You should meet regularly to tweak your plan. However, it's up to you to follow through with the plan. It's your plan, after all.

When Mary Ann came into our office, she dragged behind her a suitcase on wheels. It was filled with statements, her Trust, her paperwork, even unopened mail. Everything was in disarray. And because Andy was unable to sign anything, we had to go through a legal process with all the accounts to get them into the Trust. It took 15 months to get everything in order so that if Andy passed away, Mary Ann would be all right financially.

We even taught Mary Ann how to look into her accounts on the internet. She balked at first. She didn't want to learn everything. Now she's glad that she did. But wouldn't it be easier if she and Andy had worked together, while they were both capable, to make sure they both understood how to keep the finances in order? In Chapter 9 (on estate planning), we'll go into more issues relating to Mary Ann and Andy's situation.

No Do-Overs

What does all this mean for you? First of all, it means that if you want to avoid Sean and Tina's situation, you need to plan what you imagine doing in retirement. Not just for yourself, but with your spouse, if you have one. Make sure that you can compromise and both be happy. This is what you need to do first.

Next, find the magic *income* number you need to live the way you'd like to in retirement. Or adjust your vision of retirement to better live within your means.

Finally, commit to following through on the plans you make. And, unlike Mary Ann and Andy, make sure you both understand your finances should something happen to one of you.

Guidance on all these situations is included in our www.RetirePluggedIn.com membership site.

Retirement Assets Calculator

Our retirement assets calculator is one way to figure out approximately how much you will have at a given age when you're considering quitting work. In the asset calculator on our membership site, you can enter in what assets you have, how much you're putting in each month, your estimated interest rate or rate of return, and so on.

We recommend you use it several times, once for each pot of money, such as your 401(k), your spouse's 401(k) (which you're both contributing to), and separately for those accounts that you are *not* contributing to. You can then add them up via the sum calculator on the page to get your *total* at your projected retirement age. The calculator will allow you to figure out where you'll be financially at the age you hope to retire. This is available at www.RetirePluggedIn.com/bookdownloads.

Compatibility Questionnaire

To find out how compatible you and your spouse's goals are in retirement, go to www.RetirePluggedIn.com/bookdownloads to download a questionnaire you and your spouse can each fill out. You can then compare your answers to begin your conversation.

Plan Checkups

Retirement is not just the day you get to leave work forever. It's the beginning of a journey that has to be preplanned in great detail, at least one to five years in advance. It is just as essential to adjust the plan as you go.

One of my clients said, and it's true, "Retirement is not for the weak." There are so many moving parts that most retirees don't even realize exist. If a mistake is made, there are no do-overs like when we were kids. This is serious business.

The good news is that you're reading this book. This book will bring these moving parts to your attention. Between our membership site www.RetirePluggedIn.com and this book, you can make sure your retirement plan avoids common pitfalls so that you can have the wonderful journey you imagine.

Of course, retirement doesn't just happen in your imagination. You need to have the funds to support the lifestyle you want. In the next chapter, we'll look at how to determine whether you can retire.

2

LUMP SUM OR INCOME?

Start Your Journey with Confidence

"I've worked all my life. I don't want to do this anymore. I want more time on my own." "Can I retire? Am I going to be able to retire, ever? Can I do it today? Or do I have to wait for five years?"

These are the kinds of questions people ask because they don't know whether they're prepared. Retirement today is different than it was for your parents and your grandparents, who you may look to as examples. Your parents and grandparents most likely worked 30 years for the same company. They probably just stopped working and got a pension and some Social Security, which worked for them, since they probably didn't have a lot of extravagant plans.

But your parents and grandparents didn't expect to live as long as many of us will today, either. They became Grandma and Grandpa. They rocked the grandbabies and kind of dropped out of life. They weren't as active. Life expectancy was not that long, and health was an issue. Which brings us to **Decision #2: Do I have a lump sum or income for retirement?**

My own parents worked hard. My dad didn't have a high school education, but he got a bookkeeping certificate from a distance learning (correspondence) school. He built his own little bookkeeping business. He knew he wanted to retire one day, and he had a plan.

My father's plan was that we would move into a home that he'd purchased, and we'd stay there a while. We would then move to another house, and he'd rent that first one out. The renters would pay the mortgage. The plan was to sell the houses when he retired. My parents would put the money away and live off of it.

My father's plan was a great one at the time. Interest rates were 16%! This meant that he could sell the houses and put the money in a CD with 16% interest. My parents were bringing in $12,000 a year from that. Meanwhile, I was a college graduate and making under $4,000 a year teaching school.

I thought my parents were stone wealthy, and so did they. Well, 30 years later, $12,000 didn't go anywhere. CD rates were under 3%. My parents had to liquidate the money to live, then they sold their home. Mom and Dad passed away with less than $30,000 to their names. They had hoped to leave more to their children.

Did my parents have a plan? They did. The plan even worked well for them in the beginning. But their plan was not foolproof. They lived longer than they expected, financial trends did not continue as they hoped, and they almost ran out of money.

What we focus on in our practice is helping clients make a Life Income–Living Asset Cycle℠ plan that's going to take them all the way through retirement, and with a legacy left over for their children. Many say, "I don't need to leave anything to the kids–I raised them and paid for college." We tell them that since they can't give us their date of death, and we can't have them run out of money, there *will* be a legacy!

STARTING A NEW LIFE CHAPTER

We retire into a new chapter, a new stage of life. We imagine that we will be able to enjoy life without the time constraints we have now. However, we also worry. Can I live comfortably when my salary is gone but I still have expenses?

Some of us may still have a mortgage. What if the roof goes and we can't afford to replace it? What if the heating and air conditioning go? We don't want to put debt on credit cards. So how will we pay it off?

Maybe you've been helping your grown children financially. What if you can't help them anymore? But worst of all, what do you do if you run out of money?

But we're motivated to retire. We want to take that trip to Alaska or explore the canyons out West. Maybe we want to take a cruise and have somebody else do all the cooking while we sleep, swim, and visit places. We can even, finally, go on that missionary trip with our church.

We can do the things we've never had the time to do, like refurbishing that old car out in the garage. We can put a garden in and actually grow our own vegetables. We can volunteer and make a difference by reading to sick children at the hospital or building a home for the less fortunate with Habitat for Humanity.

We can spend more time with our grandkids and be that grandparent we never could be before, baking cookies and playing games, taking the grandkids on trips. We can see our old friends and have plenty of time now to reminisce.

Whether we plan to spend more time around home or traveling, we're eager to get started on this next chapter in our life. We want to retire, we do. But maybe we aren't sure we will ever be able to.

Patti and I have seen many clients who were certain they could never retire (and could), and others who were sure they could retire today (and really couldn't). Many of those who were afraid to retire had debt. Debt is an obstacle but not an insurmountable one.

RETIRING WITH CONFIDENCE

Can you retire? Well, first, we have to look at what your income is today. We don't mean what goes in the bank every month. We mean gross. Gross is the total amount before taxes are taken out, maybe health insurance, maybe retirement savings. Net is what goes in the bank. If we look only at the net, we're not looking at how much you really need. If you don't plan for gross, you may not have enough money.

The good news, though, is some expenses will go away when you retire. If you're contributing to your 401(k), you won't keep contributing after retirement. Maybe your commuting expenses will disappear. Maybe you'll cut the grass and clean the house instead of hiring someone to do it.

But be prepared that the health-care expense that was taken out before you ever saw your check will now have to be taken out of your money in the bank. And those health-care expenses could go up. Overall, you need to know if you have enough.

TWO EXTREMES

The couples we meet with often fall into two extremes, the over- and underconfident. The overconfident say, "I can retire today! I've got all this money. I've got a pension." Then we look at the gross income before retirement and after retirement. We look at the net income and the debts that have to be paid. Sometimes it then becomes evident that retirement isn't going to work for them at the present moment. Even though they have a decent income.

The underconfident come in and say things like, "I'm going to have to work the rest of my life. I just know it." Then we sit down with them, and we figure out what their net income is going to be. We look at their expenses and how we can put a Life Income–Living Asset Cycle℠ plan together. Sometimes, we can look at them and say, "You can retire tomorrow, and you'll be good the rest of your lives." And they smile. They can't believe it.

I'll Have to Work the Rest of My Life

One underconfident couple was Mary and John. Mary and John attended a workshop we held. They came to us thinking there was no way John could retire, but John wanted to retire badly. The commute alone was almost more than he could now handle.

Mary was the one looking at their expenses. She didn't think there was any way they could do it. She'd been doing research online about Social Security and about IRAs. She found information about how things worked, but she was confused, even though she was doing the proper research.

Mary wanted John to keep working for at least another year, but his stress at work was increasing. It was affecting his personality and his health. It was affecting their marriage.

When Mary and John came in, we started putting a Life Income–Living Asset Cycle^{SM} plan together. We looked at tax efficiency, as well as what John's pension was going to be. We calculated when they should take Social Security, what their Social Security would be, and how it would be taxed.

At their next appointment, we laid out for them on a piece of paper all their expenses down to the dollar of what they would need for John to retire, based on what they told us they wanted to accomplish. We could see them begin to picture it, to realize that they actually could do it. The whole room changed. John was ecstatic. Mary was relieved that she was not going to have to eat cat food through retirement. (Those were her actual words.)

We Can Retire Now

Bob and Sue were an example of an overconfident couple. Bob and Sue were reaching retirement age. They had wonderful jobs with big pensions. They had a huge house. Bob and Sue's problem was that they never talked to each other about finances.

Because Bob and Sue each had such good positions, they didn't think too much about household expenses. They each paid a share, but neither had a sense of the overall finances. And one of them was running up credit card debt.

When Patti and I first started working with Bob and Sue, it was very much a standoff situation. They didn't want to divulge information to each other, much less to us. Finally, Sue looked at Bob. She said, "Bob, you've got to tell me what's going on."

It turned out that Bob was supporting one of his adult children from a previous marriage. Sue had no idea. They had separate credit cards. Everything was totally separate. But he was about $16,000 in debt. This affected both of them.

So, Patti and I went through every expense with them. Then we looked at Bob and Sue: "There needs to be an adjustment, because as we sit here today, you are not able to retire." They weren't happy about that.

We also told them we could work on a Life Income–Living Asset Cycle℠ plan, if they followed the steps we outlined for the next year. They needed to get some of their bills off the table while they still had disposable income. Disposable income stops when you're on a fixed income in retirement. But they were still working, so they had time to fix this.

Still, we didn't really expect to see Bob and Sue again. But they came back six months later, and they had followed every step of our plan. They were knocking down the debt with their disposable income like we had advised.

Bob and Sue worked at it for another year. Bob retired in April 2016, and Sue's goal was to retire in December 2016. Both of them were able to achieve their goals because they started planning before they retired.

Because Bob and Sue started planning for retirement ahead of time, they were forced to face their financial realities. Until then, they had no idea how much money was going out of the house in relation to what was coming in. They saw that if they wanted to get out of the rat race, they had to make changes. And so, they diligently worked on their plan. Because they started planning early, they were able to reach their goal of retiring.

THE IMPORTANCE OF GUARANTEED INCOME

As we stated near the beginning of this chapter, Nora's parents had a plan for retirement. However, they almost ran out of money. The reason for this is they didn't have enough guaranteed income. They thought the CDs were guaranteed, but they weren't. The principal was FDIC insured, but the interest they received went down, down, down. And inflation caught up with them. Yet how do you plan for the unexpected? How can you begin the journey into retirement with confidence?

Mary thought her husband, John, couldn't retire. He would need to keep working if it killed him. Yet we showed them how everything could work together for a guaranteed income. Only then could they see their way clear.

With Bob and Sue, both were thinking, "I can just retire, and I don't have to worry about anything." Yet, by not looking at their entire financial picture, they didn't see that they couldn't afford retirement at that time. We were able to show this picture to them and also present them with an improvement plan. This way, Bob and Sue's income would be guaranteed once it became fixed in retirement.

Both couples revisited their level of confidence going into retirement. They attached their confidence level to solid numbers rather than vague hopes and fears. It took seeing how everything must work together tax-efficiently. Social Security must be maximized. Pensions must be maximized. 401(k)s must be maximized.

With all this in place, both couples were able to retire with peace of mind. They knew that they were not going to run out of money. This is what income planning is all about: getting you *through* your retirement. Because without the help of a crystal ball, no one knows your date of death.

CAN I RETIRE?

So how can you find out if you can retire, and when? The first step is to figure out exactly what your expenses are, now while you're working. Then redo the expenses for what they would be in retirement. Visit www.RetirePluggedIn.com/bookdownloads to fill out an expense worksheet that will give you the answers you need to determine when and if you can retire.

The second step is figuring out income that is guaranteed in retirement, so you don't wind up having a difficult time later on, like Nora's parents did. You want to know that you have enough money now, and also after taxes. To figure out what you might have after taxes, you can find the current tax tables at www.RetirePluggedIn.com/bookdownloads as well. The tax tables will help you figure out what your net income would be depending on your tax bracket.

The final step is what this book is all about. How do we fill that gap between what we have and what we need, if there is one? How do we plan for those contingencies we don't know might happen, like long-term health care or loss of a spouse? That's what the rest of this book is about. We'll address issues such as these in the next chapter, which focuses on Social Security.

3

SOCIAL SECURITY

Congratulations! You've Won the Lottery!

We all wish we could win the lottery instead of working to make ends meet. Like the man behind the counter at the cleaners says, "No ticket, no laundry." You can't get your cleaning back without a ticket, and you can't win the lottery without a ticket, either. Whether or not you've ever bought an actual lottery ticket, most everybody reading this book has bought one for retirement, and the winnings are guaranteed.

You probably never thought of Social Security as guaranteed lottery winnings. But when you win the lottery, you don't usually get a lump sum. You get a payout over many years, which is exactly how Social Security works. And while your chances of winning a million dollars in the lottery are five million to one, your winnings in Social Security are somewhat guaranteed.

But, like with any game, there are risks. Which brings us to **Decision #3: How and when do I claim my Social Security?** Some of us even doubt its reliability. Will Social Security continue to be there for us, or will it go broke? And what if I die before I collect it? What happens to the money? There are also rules to playing the Social Security game. If you know these rules, you can minimize any risks. You can also increase your winnings.

BASIC RULES OF THE GAME

Rule 1. You must work 40 "qualifying" quarters (or ten years) to collect Social Security. (A quarter of a year = 3 months; 3 months × 40 = 120 months, or 10 years.) You must earn a minimum amount (which changes yearly) to have a "qualifying" quarter.

Rule 2. A spouse gets a get-out-of-jail free card. This means that even if a spouse has never collected a single paycheck, they are eligible for a Social Security check worth half their spouse's "primary insurance amount" (PIA), at a minimum.

You can also think of Social Security like the game of Monopoly. It's more than just luck that allows you to get a hotel for the value of a house or buy property on the Boardwalk or Park Place. If you understand the rules and use them strategically, your money is likely to go farther. And in order to make sense of the more advanced rules, some vocabulary will also come in handy.

KEY SOCIAL SECURITY TERMS TO KNOW

PIA = Primary insurance amount. The PIA is how much you get, guaranteed, if you start collecting Social Security at your full retirement age (FRA).

FRA = Full retirement age. Your FRA is the age at which you get a guaranteed payout for the rest of your life (hopefully with cost-of-living increases).

Everyone who has worked their 40 quarters (or ten years) has a PIA at a certain age. The FRA depends on when you were born, so it's a bit more luck of the draw. For some people, the FRA may be 66, or 66 and two months, 66 and eight months, or even 67. If you look for your birthday on the chart below, you'll see your exact FRA.

Social Security Full Retirement Age (FRA)

Initiating benefits before FRA (as early as 62) may result in a decreased benefit by up to 30%, while delaying past FRA may result in an annual increase of 8% through age 70 for those born after 1942.

Year of Birth	FRA Attained
1943-1954	66
1955	66 and 2 months
1956	66 and 4 months
1957	66 and 6 months
1958	66 and 8 months
1959	66 and 10 months
1960 or later	67

Social Security Full Retirement Age (FRA) Chart

Source: Social Security Brochure EN-05-10035: "Retirement Benefits."

DETERMINING YOUR PIA AT FRA

If you register at the ssa.gov website, you can get an estimate of your PIA at FRA. On the ssa.gov website, you can see what you lose if you take Social Security early. Taking Social Security at your FRA has certain guarantees, but it is one of many options. In fact, if you're married, there are 567 ways you could claim Social Security as a couple, according to Securian Financial group. You can take Social Security earlier, if you want, but you must abide by the rules or give up part of your benefits.

Once you've gone to the ssa.gov website and seen the statistics by age for you personally, you'll need to decide if you plan to take Social Security early, at your FRA, or even later. When the best time is for you just depends. It depends on your financial needs, your stage in life, and whether you're married.

If your FRA is 66, for example, and you start taking Social Security at 62, you'll lose 25% or more of all those guaranteed lottery winnings for the rest of your life and your spouse's life.

THREE CASE STUDIES

Your guaranteed winnings can grow by as much as 8% a year from age 62 to 66 or 67. If you take Social Security early, you lose that growth, never to get it back.

Therefore, it's usually not in your best interest to take Social Security early unless you really need the money. Sometimes people might also take it if longevity doesn't run in their family and they're worried they might die soon. Sometimes people are afraid Social Security might go broke, so they think they should take what they can, while they can. Sometimes people just aren't clear on the rules.

Let's take a look at three couples who decided to take Social Security early. Each couple made a particular mistake in doing so that can easily be avoided.

Stan's Plan Backfires

Stan started collecting his Social Security at 62. He took it early because he thought Social Security was probably going to go broke.

Stan's plan was to quit his job. He'd collect some Social Security while he could and supplement what income he needed from his savings. He'd take just a year off, and he and his wife, Natasha, would be able to spend time together. His own parents had never had this time together because his dad had died early, at the age of 65.

Stan needed an income of $6,000 a month. He would get $1,500 a month from Social Security, and he had saved up money to supplement this amount. So, each month for twelve months, Stan took $4,500 out of his savings. And you know what? Stan and Natasha had a wonderful year.

After the year, Stan figured he'd get a less stressful job. After all, he had Social Security now, so he could earn less money. The only thing was, not long after he went back to work, Social Security just stopped one month.

It stopped because of the earnings test exempt amount. Stan just couldn't understand what had happened! The rule he didn't know about says that if you collect Social Security *before* Full Retirement Age, which Stan did, and you earn *over* the "earnings test exempt amount," which he did, they're going to subtract $1 from your benefits for every $2 *more* you earn! In 2022, the earnings test exempt amount was $19,650/year.

Basically, since Stan was making $4,500 a month, in less than a year he'd lost 100% of his Social Security. And Natasha didn't have her 40 quarters, so she didn't collect a benefit. And now neither of them had Social Security.

Not only that, but Stan had locked in a lower payment he wasn't even getting. He couldn't reverse this because you only have one year to reverse your decision. Stan had no idea this could happen. He didn't know the rules, and what he didn't know hurt him. We'll revisit Stan and Natasha later in the chapter.

Fred Collects, Saves His IRA

Fred and Peg had been married over 40 years. Fred was an executive of a large firm. He was six years older than Peg, and he earned a lot more money. Both put away as much as they could in their 401(k)s and had well over a million dollars in retirement accounts. Fred also had a pension.

When Fred turned 66, he said, "Hey, I'm gonna take my Social Security because I'm 66 and that's my FRA." So, Fred took his Social Security. He got $2,600 a month. He also had his pension.

Between his Social Security and his pension, Fred figured he would not have to take much from his IRA. They could live off Social Security and his pension and save the IRA for a rainy day.

What Fred didn't know was that his Social Security would be guaranteed to grow 8% a year, even *after* he reached his FRA. So, when he started collecting, he cut off that increase. This also meant that if Fred passed away, Peg would not get that higher amount of Social Security either. The higher Social Security would have given his wife higher income and cost-of-living raises for the rest of her life, even if he predeceased her.

Even if they got 8% on the IRA money, they would never catch up with the 8% increase in Social Security income. This is because of how Social Security is taxed in comparison to IRAs. IRAs are 100% taxable at both the federal and state level. No more than 85% of your Social Security is taxed federally and, in most states, it isn't taxed at all by the state. (You can download a list of states that tax Social Security at www.RetireUnlocked/bookdownloads.)

What happened here is that Fred and Peg didn't calculate the long-range benefit of maxing out that Social Security. They didn't know about the increases. They didn't know that you didn't have to pay taxes on the full amount. Because of all they did not know, Fred and Peg did not reap the maximum benefit of their lottery winnings. We'll revisit what they could have done a little later.

Jack Collects While Millie Works

Our third couple, Millie and Jack, met in high school. They never went to college. They lived frugally their entire lives. Jack worked hard, and Millie kept the home fires burning. She never really had a job outside of the house, so they didn't have as much savings as the other two couples.

Jack and Millie guessed that the only guaranteed income they'd have in retirement was Jack's Social Security because Millie had never worked 40 quarters. In their favor, they didn't have any outstanding debt. They'd done a great job paying off the house over 30 years and of raising two self-sufficient children who lived within their means.

To have a better future, Millie decided to work a low-paying job. She wanted to make those 40 quarters, so she could get Social Security too.

Jack decided he'd take Social Security at his FRA and continue to work. Then he'd have enough money to max out his 401(k). Between ages 66 and 70, Jack was able to put the maximum amount into his 401(k) because he received Social Security.

Well, congratulations to Jack and Millie on planning to live within their means! And also to Jack for thinking about Millie's future if he predeceased her. He wanted to put more away in that 401(k) just in case Millie needed it. But again, what they didn't know could have significantly helped them.

It was a great idea to put more money into their retirement for later, but just like Fred, Jack was giving up an 8% a year increase in Social Security by taking it at his FRA instead of age 70—even though he was working until 70 anyway. It just seemed like a good idea to put more money into the 401(k).

Meanwhile, Millie was working hard to get her 40 quarters without knowing that she was already eligible for half of Jack's PIA at FRA for Social Security. *Even if she never worked.* Social Security would either give her half of his Social Security, or what she qualified for with her 40 quarters working a low-paying job. Of course, she'd take the higher payment! At least the extra savings would come in handy, right?

What both Millie and Jack also didn't know about was something called provisional income. Provisional Income is the calculation that determines how much of your Social Security is taxed federally (0%, 50%, or 85%). If you plan for this, you can reduce your taxes. Millie and Jack were wrecking their future provisional income by putting more money into their 401(k). We'll come back to their scenario and the outcome at the end of the chapter.

SO, WHEN SHOULD I TAKE SOCIAL SECURITY?

Looking at our three couples, you might think that everyone should wait as long as they can to collect Social Security. Well, absolutely not! If a working couple both earn benefits, why not wait until both of them are 70? Well, here is the basic Social Security rule for a married couple: if one spouse dies, the survivor gets to keep the larger check.

But there is a catch. If one spouse passes away and they haven't collected the smaller Social Security check yet, nobody ever collects even one $1 from it! That money is gone.

This is why we often recommend something we call the 62–70 strategy. This simply means if you're married and you both have good incomes, then one of you may want to take your Social Security as early as possible, either 62 or by 66 (depending on how long you plan to work). The other spouse then waits to get the highest amount possible, at age 70. The higher amount will be there for either one of you no matter how long you live, but if one of you passes away and neither has collected, nobody gets that second check.

What if you're not married? Well again, it depends. If people in your family have been living into their 90s, you'll likely need money for a long time. You're going to want to max that out as best you can. However, you have to determine how long it will take to get those monthly benefits back if you don't take it.

Let's say your FRA is 66. If you wait until 70, you have given up four years of income from Social Security. Take Jim as an example. Jim could get $2,434 a month at 66, or $3,345 a month at 70. If he waits until 70, he's lost 48 months, or $116,000. It would take Jim 128 months, or almost 11 years, to get that money back.

However, if Jim lives into his 90s, he not only gets back his $116,000, he gets an additional $109,000 plus increased cost-of-living adjustments! Those are called "break-even calculations." What does it take to break even? You should calculate this before you make a decision.

Other Rules

Are there any other rules you need to know? Absolutely. For instance, did you know that Medicare premiums are affected when you collect Social Security? This is because Social Security affects how much income you have on your tax return.

There's also the Budget Bill of 2015 that took $40,000 out of the pocket of most couples who are dual earners. However, there are certain birth dates that can escape that rule. You just need to know what they are. As mentioned earlier, a couple could collect Social Security 567 different ways, and all of these ways have rules.

Yet the Social Security Administration forbids employees from giving advice or explaining these rules to you. Like the IRS, if an employee gives you a wrong answer, the larger administration is not responsible. It's your problem. Let's take a deeper look at how some of this works by revisiting our three case studies.

THREE CASE STUDIES REVISITED

A Better Plan for Stan and Natasha

If you recall, Stan's father died at 65. Stan didn't want to die at his desk and miss out on retirement and spending quality time with his wife, like his father did. So, Stan took his Social Security at 62. He spent a wonderful year with Natasha, but with the Social Security "earnings test" he lost 100% of his Social Security while he was working and had not yet reached his FRA.

Natasha ended up going to work, and now they were both working stressful jobs. They were worse off than before Stan retired. They knew their retirement savings would have to supplement what meager Social Security Stan might earn back. They were petrified about their future.

So, what else could Stan have done?

First of all, at 62, Stan was not ready for full retirement. Stan wasn't looking at his situation rationally. He didn't take into consideration important facts like how much his father smoked. Stan's father had never taken care of himself, while Stan and Natasha made health-wise choices. So, Stan didn't have such a great a chance of dying at 65.

Stan could have taken some time off work, maybe even found a lesser-paying job earlier. He could have supplemented the pay from this job with a little bit from his IRA and delayed taking Social Security. Stan didn't want to work until 70, but you can stop working *before* you collect Social Security. He could have taken money from his savings in the meantime, then taken Social Security at 70. Then they would have had much more money to live on for the rest of their lives, with increases for inflation!

The real shock to them was that Natasha didn't need 40 quarters to collect Social Security. Because she was married to Stan, she could collect half of his PIA while he collected *all* of his PIA. If she had done this, and Stan waited to collect at 70, they would've had $50,000 a year from Social Security.

But even more surprising to them, the provisional income calculation determines how much taxes are due on your Social Security. The table below shows the calculation for provisional income and how much of your Social Security is taxable.

Social Security Taxable Portion

Provisional Income (AGI + Nontaxable Interest + ½ of Social Security Benefit) above the below amounts may result in a portion of social security benefits being taxable.

Single Filers	Joint Filers	Amount Taxable
Below $25,000	Below $32,000	0%
$25,000-$34,000	$32,000-$44,000	50%
Above $34,000	Above $44,000	85%

Social Security Taxable Portion

Source: ssa.gov/benefits/retirement/planner/taxes.html

Provisional income counts only *half* of their total Social Security benefit. Half of their total Social Security benefits would be $25,000 for Stan and Natasha together because they are collecting $50,000 a year. They are under the provisional income tax bracket of $32,000 for a couple.

They would've had $50,000 a year tax-free the rest of their lives, and with inflation increases! That *would* have been like winning the lottery. In fact, $50,000 a year is the equivalent of having $1 million in an account earning 5%. Stan and Natasha had no idea that they were giving up that much.

A Better Option for Fred and Peg

Fred and Peg both worked hard and put a lot of money away in their 401(k)s. At age 66, Fred took his Social Security and his pension. Peg, who was six years younger, planned to wait to take her Social Security until 66 because they really didn't need the income. They seemed set. Yet they could have made their future even better.

It seemed really smart to take Social Security and let the IRA money grow, but was it? Social Security would've grown by a guaranteed compound annual rate of 8% each year it was deferred until age 70. The Social Security would be less taxable for the rest of their lives than the IRA money they were putting away. Plus, there wasn't any guarantee their IRA money would grow at that high of a rate or that it would last. Social Security is guaranteed the rest of your life.

If Fred had instead supplemented his pension from his IRA until he turned 70, he would not have had as much in his IRA account. This would actually have benefited them. This is because, when you reach the magic age of 72 (changed from 70.5 by the SECURE Act of 2019, which went into effect in 2020), you *must* take out required minimum distributions (RMDs).

Because they put all this money away, and didn't touch it, their RMDs would be higher. And so would their taxes. In addition, if Peg had taken her Social Security at 62 and Fred had waited until 70, they could have better maximized their Social Security income.

Now, let's revisit our last couple, Millie and Jack.

If Jack Had Just Waited

Millie and Jack were high school sweethearts. They'd worked hard but didn't have as many opportunities as the other two couples did. They weren't able to save a lot of money, but they did have a plan. Jack would take Social Security at his FRA. He'd continue to work, and he'd put more money from his paycheck into his 401(k).

Jack's Social Security was $1,350 a month. That allowed him to max out his 401(k) at $2,000 a month. That was unbelievable for them. They could never have afforded this without the Social Security. From ages 66 to 70, Jack put $24,000 a year into their 401(k). That was $100,000 additional savings!

They thought this was the smartest thing they could do. Millie did her part by going to work so she could build up credits to collect Social Security.

So, how could they have done better? Well, although it's a great idea to put more money into their retirement account for later, Jack was giving up that 8% a year increase for himself and Millie's future income. Remember, if Jack predeceases Millie, she gets to keep the higher amount.

His Social Security at age 70 would've been $1,850. That's an additional $500 a month, or $6,000 a year.

Also remember that Social Security income is not taxed as high as IRA income. How much would he have to take out of his IRA to equal $6,000 in Social Security income? Well, because the IRA is fully taxable, if he wanted that additional $6,000 a year, he'd have to take out $8,000 to get the $6,000 he would've gotten from his Social Security.

Can Jack guarantee $8,000 a year for life from the $100,000 he saved? Can he increase that for cost of living? His IRA will eventually run out of money. His Social Security wouldn't have.

Millie was also working hard to get her 40 quarters, never realizing she was eligible for half of Jack's FRA Social Security. Millie will get half of $1,350, or $675. She'll never earn enough on her own to equal that. But without knowing all this, she was working harder than she needed to for something she already had.

They also wrecked their taxes with the higher RMDs from their 401(k). If Jack had waited to collect Social Security, he would have had no state income tax where they lived, and little to no federal income tax on it. Their combined benefit would have been $30,000 a year. And due to provisional income rules, there would be no tax. They would've had the equivalent of about $40,000 a year guaranteed income, with a much higher survivor benefit if Jack predeceased Millie.

JUST THE TIP OF THE ICEBERG

These stories touch just the tip of the iceberg of Social Security planning, which could be an entire book itself. These three couples did an excellent job of planning based on the knowledge they had. However, what they didn't know did hurt them. They didn't understand the rules and regulations around Social Security. They didn't understand the basics of how Social Security is taxed versus IRAs, and how RMDs from IRAs worked.

The likelihood they could get all this information on their own is small. That's why we created the www.RetirePluggedIn.com website. These rules are all explained to members. Our membership site is dedicated to not only educating those heading toward retirement but also to alerting those in retirement about information applicable to them right as they reach a crucial age at which they need to make a critical decision. The membership site provides independent information not slanted toward anybody's interest but yours. To get an idea of what such a membership would provide, go to www.RetirePluggedIn.com and watch the video introduction on the home page.

You get only one opportunity to maximize your Social Security and make those guaranteed lottery winnings pay off. Once you start collecting, it's too late to make changes. As complex as Social Security is, it is just the beginning of retirement planning. In the next chapter, we'll address what could be the greatest threat to your retirement, if you get it wrong: health care.

4

HEALTH CARE

The Greatest Threat to Your Retirement

Alice and her husband, Bruce, sat in front of us. Alice was holding back tears. This was how worried she was about health care and her future. Her mother had developed Alzheimer's disease at age 58 and lived until 71. Alice had wanted to keep her mother at home, but 24-hour care was out of the question.

Instead, her mother's last nine years were spent in a horrible nursing home that still cost $10,000 a month. If her mother hadn't inherited $1.5 million from her uncle, they couldn't have paid for it.

Now Alice's mother was gone, and so was the money. "I don't have that kind of money, so what if something like that happens to me? They tell me it's genetic. Would I get help through Medicare?"

The answer was not what Alice wanted to hear. No, Medicare does not pay for long-term care. Cognitive care is also not covered by Medicare. Cognitive care would be needed if you have mental decline, dementia, or Alzheimer's disease. Medicare only pays for health care, such as a medical procedure or a hospital stay. Medicare does not provide help with the "activities of daily living," or ADLs, as they call them.

Basic tasks like bathing fall in the category of ADLs. Other activities include dressing, eating, toileting (going to the bathroom by yourself), continence, or moving from a bed to a chair. According to the federal government, if a person needs help with two out of six of these activities of daily living, this person needs long-term care. And Medicare does not cover it.

So, what do you do if you need long-term care? This is **Decision #4: How do I prepare for a long-term care need?**

Alice made sure to purchase a Medicare supplement. She bought F (which will not be available in 2022), she told us, the most comprehensive one.

But there is no Medicare supplement, or Medigap policy, as they call it, that pays for long-term care. A supplement only covers the "gaps" of what Medicare covers, such as deductibles, co-pays, and "excess charges." Medicare doesn't cover long-term care, therefore neither does your Medicare supplement or Medigap policy!

MEDICAID

Alice was desperate at this point. "My friend Robin took care of her mother at home. But when her mother got really bad, she got her into a facility and I thought Medicare paid for it. 'Medi-something' paid for it, anyway."

"Medicaid?" we suggested.

Medicaid is a benefit for those people who are very poor. At one time, it was easy enough for retirees to get Medicaid benefits by putting all their assets under their children's names. This way they'd look poor on paper.

But Medicaid caught on. The government now has a look-back period when you sign up for Medicaid. They actually look back through your records to see if you gave any money away during the five-year preceding period.

Sometimes people who would otherwise not be eligible still get Medicaid by doing some sophisticated planning with a "Medicaid specialist" who knows the complex rules. But if Medicaid finds out that you actually should *not* have qualified, that is considered Medicaid fraud, which the government takes very seriously. Even if you do legitimately qualify with some serious planning, they can come back to reclaim money paid out on your behalf by Medicaid.

Medicaid offers incentives for every state to recover not only as much wrongfully awarded money as it can but also any money that can be gotten from the patient's estate through a lien on the home or other assets. Medicaid will actually go to the children, or whoever the retirees hid their money with, and take from them the money paid out by Medicaid.

So, what do you do if you get Alzheimer's, dementia, Parkinson's, ALS, or some other long-term condition? This is a realistic fear. The Administration on Aging at LongTermCare.gov states that "someone turning age 65 today has almost a 70% chance of needing some type of long-term care services and supports in their remaining years." And, according to Genworth 2020 Cost of Care survey, the average annual cost for a semi-private room in a facility is $93,075. A private room is $105,850 annually.

Alice's husband, Bruce, said, "Honey, don't worry. I'll always be here for you, no matter what. I'll take care of you."

But what if something happens to Bruce? What if he can't physically take care of Alice 24 hours a day?

LIVING IN DENIAL

Even though the odds are against them, many people live in denial of the statistics. It won't happen to me or my spouse. We'll be part of that 30% who won't need care! Sharon and Henry were one such couple. Henry was a Vietnam War veteran, which we see a lot of.

We shared with them that there is a 70% chance of needing long-term care. Henry said he would solve that problem with a 32-cent bullet. He wouldn't wind up in a nursing home!

Well, Henry developed dementia. Fortunately, he didn't remember his plan with the bullet, but it meant that Sharon had to take care of him. Henry didn't know where he was, or who Sharon was. He would become agitated and even physical because of the disorientation, which could be a problem when reliving his memories of the Vietnam War. In addition, "sundowning" struck. Like babies, those with dementia often mix up night and day, so Sharon would be up all night with him.

It became more than Sharon could handle. She eventually had to put Henry in a facility. When Henry went into this facility, the nurses told Sharon that he depended upon her visits. He wouldn't even sleep unless she were there. So, Sharon spent all day with Henry, then would go home and fall in bed, to get up and do it all again the next day.

Meanwhile, Henry's military pension of $6,000 a month was going directly to the nursing facility. They had lived on Henry's pension and Sharon's small Social Security check for years. Sharon now had to take money out of her savings to pay the bills at home.

Don't Count on the VA

Henry was a veteran, but he wasn't getting help from the United States Department of Veteran Affairs (VA). Many veterans think the VA will take care of them. That was true years ago, because years ago the VA had beds for people who were disabled. Mostly, these were elderly people. But today, thank goodness, we have wonderful medical advances.

And with the advances, all those young soldiers fighting in Afghanistan and Iraq are more likely to come back alive but disabled. In fact, according to the National Center for Veterans Analysis and Statistics, as of May 2019, "The Veteran population has been declining since 1990 while the number of veterans with a service-connected disability has risen 117%." So, there are now far fewer beds available for the elderly disabled.

There is the Veterans Aid and Attendance Benefit, which reduces the cost of care for veterans and surviving spouses who require assisted living. The benefit provides a maximum supplement of $3,261 a month (as of 2022) for home care, but as of September 2018, there was also a "five-year look back" period on assets to qualify (similar to the Medicaid qualification) because your net worth, outside the value of your home, can be no more than $138,489 as of 2022. We strongly urge you to get competent financial counsel before applying.

Don't Count on TRICARE

When Henry went into the care facility, Sharon didn't call us right away. She didn't think he would be there long. And once he passed away, she figured, she'd call us to find out how to do the plan we set up for her. Well, four months went by, and Sharon started getting alarmed. Not only was all of Henry's pension going toward his care, but her savings were dwindling too.

Sharon finally called and asked us the usual question. "Why isn't Medicare paying for this?" She also asked about TRICARE, since as a veteran, Henry had "TRICARE for Life." TRICARE is a wonderful health plan that costs nothing and covers everything in health care for retired military. Except, TRICARE only pays *if* Medicare pays, just like a Medigap policy.

It used to be if you had TRICARE, you didn't need Medicare. The rule has changed now. You *must* have Medicare Parts A and B to be eligible for TRICARE. If veterans do not take Medicare Part A (which is free) and purchase Medicare Part B, they will be dropped from TRICARE at age 65. We were back to the same problem. This facility care was *not* health care. It was long-term care for loss of two of six ADLs. It was therefore not eligible for payment from Medicare, and therefore not TRICARE either.

Another Option

We explained to Sharon about another benefit that she was not aware of called VA Aid and Attendance, which we mentioned earlier. This benefit allowed anyone who had been in the military during a wartime period to get a supplemental benefit. It didn't matter whether they participated in the war or not. The maximum benefit for 2022 was $3,261/month, and even that would be a great help for Sharon. She applied for it, and now she's currently waiting. It takes a while to be approved.

When we plan our finances, we have to plan not just for retirement now but also for the fourth stage in life: frailty or disability. If you took care of yourself, if you exercised and didn't smoke, you may be less likely to die if you have a heart attack, a stroke, or even cancer.

In the past, people were not so healthy. They more commonly died from such things. Add to that the amazing medical advances being discovered every day. So now, we tend to live past these things and be incapacitated. Or we live long enough to become old and frail.

So, retiring means that you must address these things. There is more to it than long-term care. There's also regular medical care. Most people think, "I shouldn't have a problem. I'll have Medicare." Well, that's not the full story. Medicare is extremely complicated, and coverage doesn't start until you hit 65.

SANDRA AND PETER'S HEALTH INSURANCE GAP

Peter thought he had enough money saved, so he retired at 62. He knew he'd have to pay for health insurance since he'd lose his coverage through work. What he didn't know was that his rate would increase dramatically from the $600 a month he paid for health insurance through his employer. It would cost Peter about $2,000 a month to pay for the same plan on his own.

Peter said, "I cannot afford $24,000 year. What am I going to do?"

We told him that he had a few choices. One was to go back to work. Another was to risk not having insurance for a few years.

Peter couldn't take that risk. He tried to go back to work, but they had eliminated his position. There was no place for him to go back to. So, Sandra went to work at a low-paying job just to get benefits to cover them.

Peter felt bad that he had let Sandra down. He was depressed, thinking that he should have just worked another three years. Peter thought that if he waited to retire until he and Sandra were both 65, they'd be set. They'd be totally covered. Well, even that's not exactly true.

Medicare Complications and Supplements

We think Medicare is going to cover us. But Medicare is not so straightforward. You may need to have a Medicare supplement, or Medigap policy, to cover certain things. There is Medicare A for the hospital. Medicare B for the doctors. Medicare A is free (*if* you've paid sufficiently into Social

Security). Medicare B is never free. And Medicare B benefits depend on your income. The higher your income, the higher the premium. Current premiums as of this writing are in the chart on page 111 of the book. The more you make, the more you pay. It gets very complicated.

You have roughly a seven-month window when you turn 65 to take Medicare. This window opens three months before you turn 65 and includes the month of your 65th birthday. The window closes three months after. If you miss that window, there's a penalty added to your premium for life. And if you don't take Medicare in coordination with your Social Security correctly, there are penalties as well.

For basic full coverage, you need Medicare A, B, and a Medigap policy. If you look on the internet to buy a Medicare supplement policy, you will see Medicare supplements, or Medigap policies A, B, C, and D (no E), limited availability in 2021 of F or F high deductible, G, K, I, L, M, and N. In addition, there are "Medicare Advantage" plans that include the supplement, Medicare Part B and D. These are sold touting many additional benefits, such as lower Part B costs, vision, and dental, but *be careful*, because you'll give up your right to switch back to original Medicare and a supplement, and your ability to see any provider or specialist you wish. So, how do you know which one to take?

At this point, Peter said, "This is giving me a headache. A and B should be all we need."

We wish it were that easy! Even if Peter chose a great Medigap policy to supplement their Medicare, neither Medicare nor Medigap covers prescriptions! We explained to Peter he also needed Part D, which is a prescription policy.

"Thank goodness we're healthy!" Peter responded. "We don't need any prescriptions, so I can probably skip that!"

But if Peter didn't buy it, even though he didn't need it, he would have a penalty for every month he delayed purchasing Medicare. Medicare multiplies 1% of the "national base beneficiary premium" ($33.37 in 2022) times the number of full uncovered months you didn't have Part D or creditable coverage and adds that to your premium. And that penalty is for life! And the prescription policies, believe it or not, don't cover all prescriptions. Different policies cover different prescriptions in different amounts.

You used to be able to go to your local pharmacist and find out which of your prescriptions were covered by which company, but they're no longer allowed to tell you!

Now you must go to medicare.gov and go to the tab at the top called "Drug Coverage (Part D)" to find out what prescriptions are covered, and to what extent by *each company*, and do the comparisons yourself! The new coverages are posted for the next year in the last quarter of the current year. In 2021, the open enrollment was scheduled to be October 15, 2021, through December 7, 2021, for the year 2022. That is an "open window" that you can switch to get better coverage for your prescriptions. Miss the window? No "do-overs" in retirement! You'll have to wait until the next year.

Peter was at least relieved to learn that he wouldn't be paying more than about $600 a month for both of them. "And that's going to completely cover us?"

"Well, it's not going to cover long-term care."

The Long-Term Care Problem

Peter had heard that long-term care insurance premiums were really high. He was right. He'd also heard that they periodically raise them. He was right about that too. We have actually seen premiums go up 90% in one year.

Long-term care is such a problem that the federal government has now encouraged insurance companies to start new programs. There are now hybrid long-term care and life insurance policies. There are long-term care and annuity hybrids, where you can reposition some money, get coverage, and not have premiums every year. There are even partnership programs that include a short long-term care policy, with some Medicaid help.

Another option, which is really, really good, is called short-term care. It only covers one year, but it actually covers rehab, whereas long-term care doesn't. So, if you break a hip, you go to the hospital and Medicare covers it. But if you go to rehab, Medicare only fully covers you if you're "improving" by their standards, and only up to 20 days; then (as of the time of this writing) you have a $194.50/day deductible until 100 days (for 2022), when Medicare stops completely. The short-term care policy will cover that rehab.

GETTING STARTED WITH YOUR PLAN

People tell us all the time that they never knew it was so difficult to retire. Health care may just be the most difficult part, especially putting in place a long-term care plan. So, what do you do? How do you get started?

If all of this seems overwhelming, it can be extremely helpful to find someone impartial who can give you an explanation of each Medicare supplement, as well as care options. Then you can figure out which is best for you. "Insurance professionals" will be knocking on your door when you turn 65. They get mailing lists, and you'll be bombarded with offers from Medicare supplements. No explanation, just whatever they're selling. These sellers are not impartial.

If you don't have a truly independent, knowledgeable advisor who can explain all your options to you, you can go to the final chapter of this book to find out how to get one. You can also go to www.RetirePluggedIn.com and join as a member. On the membership site, we go beyond the basics outlined in this book so you can find out what you really need to know. As a member of www.RetirePluggedIn.com you will be alerted each year when the coverages are posted and receive information about how to compare them.

In the next chapter, we'll go into qualified money and the IRS rules that can make it so difficult. We'll examine plenty of mistakes others have made, so you can see where they went wrong and avoid making these mistakes yourself.

5

IRS RULES FOR QUALIFIED MONEY

Is My Money Qualified?

Fully updated for the SECURE Act and the CARES Act!

REQUIRED MINIMUM DISTRIBUTIONS (RMDS)

Required Minimum Distributions (RMDs) are laws that force you to take money out of your IRA (or other retirement accounts) and pay taxes!

SECURE Act Effective January 1, 2020

The SECURE Act has significantly changed planning for your IRAs! Shirley turned 70.5 on December 23, 2019. It's important to note that the SECURE Act does *not* change RMDs for her, because if you were 70.5 *before* January 1, 2020, you must continue using the "old RMD rules." To learn how the SECURE Act may affect you, go to www.RetirePluggedIn.com/bookdownloads to find an outline of the main parts of the SECURE Act.

CARES Act Effective March 21, 2020

Due to the coronavirus (COVID-19) pandemic, the CARES Act eliminated RMDs for the year 2020, based on the 2019 end of year values, because of the hardship it might cause retirees. RMDs are calculated on the value of your retirement account on December 31 of the prior year. Because 2019 was the highest values in the historic bull market since 2009, the end of year values looked great! However, the market in the beginning of 2021 tumbled over 30%, making retirees take out a disproportionate amount for their RMDs in 2021. Any time the prior end-of-year values are high, and then the stock market drops in the new year, RMD rules force you to take out based on the higher value even though you've already lost the money! The everchanging rules will make it very difficult to calculate your RMD for 2022 because the SECURE Act *also* changed the rules, and the IRS is contemplating changing it further! The CARES Act features will be updated as needed on the www.RetirePluggedIn.com/bookdownloads page.

The Third Leg of Retirement Income

Qualified money is the third leg on the famous stool of retirement that includes pensions, Social Security, and IRAs or 401(k)s. Qualified money is the money in our retirement accounts, often known as IRAs, 401(k)s, 403(b)s, 457s, 401(a)s, SEPs, and SIMPLEs, and the names go on. Regardless of the type of account, all qualified money comes under a set of special rules with the IRS since taxes have likely been deferred on the accounts. Which brings us to **Decision #5: How do I use my qualified money most tax-efficiently?**

For many of us, qualified money is the largest asset outside of our homes and what we will depend on in retirement. So, if you don't know the tax rules, you could be risking your retirement.

One of our clients, Shirley, did not know the rules. Shirley had enough income to live on. She had a pension from her deceased husband and a good amount of Social Security. Shirley didn't need to touch her IRA, that third leg on her retirement stool of income, even when she turned the magic age of 70.5 (now age 72, due to the SECURE Act, as of January 1, 2020), the age for RMDs.

On her 70 and one-half birthday, Shirley was required by law to take out something called required minimum distributions (RMDs). You see, the government had already figured out her statistical date of death.

The IRS has a chart listing how many years you're likely going to live once you turn 70.5. They've calculated out how many years you're likely going to live beyond 71, 72, 73, and so on because the IRS wants you to liquidate your qualified money before you die. They want to get their taxes.

But since Shirley never touched her IRA, she never thought about it. When she turned 70.5, she did nothing. The next year, she went to do her taxes (at the last minute, April 2), and her tax person said, "Shirley, did you take your required minimum distribution? I see here that you have a large IRA."

"No, no," Shirley said. "I don't need to take anything out. I'm living fine." Her tax person then explained that she *had* to take out RMDs. The government had determined that she had 27.4 years more to live, so they wanted her to divide her account value on December 31 of the prior year by 27.4 and take out that much money. Otherwise, there would be a penalty.

"Oh, well, I didn't do it." Shirley didn't think it would be that big of a deal. "So, what's the penalty?" Shirley's IRA was at $1 million, and 27.4 was the "factor" for age 70—$1 million divided by 27.4 is a $36,496.35 RMD. If Shirley didn't take that amount out, her penalty would be 50% of $36,496.35, or $18,248.18, *and* she would still have to take the $36,496.35 out and pay taxes on it! Shirley really lost out on another front, because the first year that RMDs are due, you have until April 1 of the next year to take the RMD out, but she visited her tax person on April 2!

Luckily, Shirley's tax person knew that she could submit a request for a waiver due to reasonable cause. If she didn't have a tax person who knew that, she would have had to pay that 50%. So, it is important to have a tax person who knows the IRS laws specific to retirement.

However, there's still a good chance Shirley won't get the waiver because there was not "reasonable cause." She wasn't sick. She wasn't traveling. She just didn't do it.

What can you learn from Shirley's story? For one, it's a good idea to find a tax person who is well aware of IRS laws regarding qualified money, especially if you're attempting to plan for your retirement on your own. It is of the utmost importance that you *know* and follow the IRS rules and regulations. The rules are many and always changing, so it's important to stay up to date. For instance, the age for RMDs has been the same, 70.5, since 1975, but it changed to 72 with the passage of the SECURE Act, as of January 1, 2020, *unless* you were already required to take RMDs because you turned 70.5 by December 31, 2019. If you don't follow these rules, consequences can be severe, as examples throughout this chapter will further demonstrate.

Now, let's look at the common account types for qualified money.

COMMON ACCOUNT TYPES

Whether a 401(k), an IRA, or one of a number of government plans, all of these qualified accounts work very much the same. They are deferred, which means that the amount is tax deductible the year you put the money in. The money also grows tax deferred. This means that these accounts are also 100% taxable, federal and state, when the money comes out, including the growth. If you take the money out before age 59 and a half, you also pay a 10% penalty, unless you meet certain requirements at age 55.

401(k)

A 401(k) is an account set up by your employer for you to defer part of your salary. This is usually pretax money. You sign up, and you say you want 2%, 6%, or so on of your salary to go into this account before you get your paycheck. You won't pay taxes on this money now, so it's almost like the government is subsidizing your retirement account.

As of 2022, those under 50 can put away $19,500 a year, tax deferred, into a 401(k). This means you get a tax deduction each year. If you're over 50, you can put in an extra $6,500 a year "catch-up," for a total of $26,000 a year. Many people are unable to put much away when they're young. But once their kids are grown and out of college, people can often take advantage of the higher contribution limit.

You may also have a Roth 401(k) option at work. A Roth 401(k) allows you to contribute "after-tax" money (you pay the taxes now) into the plan, and it will grow tax-free forever! This is a great option for future planning if you can pay the taxes. It follows the same contribution limits as the traditional 401(k), and your combined traditional and Roth contributions cannot exceed the maximums of $19,500 or $26,000, depending on your age. If you choose the Roth 401(k) option, be sure to learn all the rules about withdrawals, as they can be complicated.

The good news is also that many companies, as well as the federal government, will match a portion of what you contribute. This increases your retirement savings!

IRA

You don't have to put money into an IRA through an employer. But you do have to put in money that has been "earned"—in other words, not from your Social Security, pension, rental income, and so on. In 2022, those under 50 can contribute as much as $6,000 a year into an IRA. Those over 50 can contribute up to $7,000 a year. If the money is pretax, then this could become a tax deduction, depending on your income and whether you have an employer retirement account available.

Government Plans

The same kinds of plans exist for people who work for the government. Federal employees have what is called a Thrift Savings Plan, or TSP, which has the same rules as a 401(k). If you work for a county, you probably have either a 403(b), which has the same rules as the 401(k), or a 457, which is a government deferral as well.

TAX LAWS WHEN COMBINING ACCOUNTS

It's not uncommon to have more than one type of retirement account, or more than one 401(k). Maybe you worked at a school that had a 403(b), then got a different job and had a 401(k). But you do need to be aware of the tax laws governing the transfer of funds if you want to combine accounts.

Take Richard, for example. He had three 401(k)s from different companies he'd worked for over his career. So, Richard decided to move his 401(k)s together into one account. He had one large 401(k), and two smaller accounts, so he decided to ask the smaller accounts to send him the money. He would put the money they sent him in the big one. Then he'd have all his money in one place.

Well, the problem was, when Richard asked for the money, he didn't ask them to *transfer* the money. He asked them to send *him* the money. Well, much to his surprise, they took out 20% in taxes when they sent him the money because, by law, they must. A *transfer* sends the money from the custodian (institution that holds the account) to another custodian to hold the account for you. The check is *not* written to you, but to the institution "FBO," *for your benefit.*

The law requires that if the qualified employer plan sends a check directly payable to you from the plan, they must automatically withhold 20% federal taxes. If, instead, the check goes to another qualified plan, such as an IRA or another employer plan, it's a nontaxable transfer and nothing is withheld.

So, when Richard went to add this money to his larger 401(k), his first problem was that he had to replace the 20% they withheld and sent to the IRS. He had to add it from his own funds to rollover (transfer without taxes) the whole amount. If he didn't, it would be considered a "taxable distribution." Let's say his 401(k) had $50,000, and they withheld 20% ($10,000). If Richard didn't have $10,000 in the bank to replace it, he would owe taxes on the $10,000, even though he didn't receive it in his own hands.

The second and bigger problem is that he didn't do it once, but twice!

So, why is that a problem? Well, as of 2015, there's a new law that says you can only take the money in your hand and then move it to another qualified account once in a 12-month period. If you do it twice, all the affected IRAs are no longer IRAs. All of the affected qualified accounts are now 100% taxable! Richard did not know that.

If we don't know these rules, we risk losing our qualified money, or life savings, to the taxman in retirement. Qualified money is the key to a peaceful retirement, a secure retirement, a worry-free retirement. We want to keep as much of that money as we can.

Accumulating the money is simple enough when it is taken automatically out of our paychecks. Sometimes we are even fortunate enough to have an employer match. Whoa, free money! That's wonderful. It's when we take it out that things get complicated.

DECUMULATION AND TAXES

Accumulating money in our qualified accounts happens almost like magic. Our money goes in every month, and hey, the market went down, but hey, when it came up, I made a lot of money! Everything worked out. The system is set up so it's almost impossible for us to fail in accumulating money. But we can easily fail at decumulating it.

Joseph is an example of this. He was very careful to live within his means. He never spent his qualified money. And, like Shirley, when he hit 70.5, the IRS wanted their due. Thus, at 70.5, Joseph took money out based on the 27.4 factor. This amounted to 3.65% of his qualified money.

Now, that wouldn't have been a problem if Joseph hadn't also deferred his Social Security. So, when he reached 70.5, Joseph's income went up by $3,500 a month from Social Security. It went up another $3,500 a month from his IRA. His taxes went through the roof! He even had to pay more for his Medicare premium because Medicare premiums have an "income related monthly adjustment amount" (IRMAA). He had no idea that would happen.

Like Joseph, many of us don't really know how this all works. You see, when you put money in every month, you're "dollar-cost averaging." This means that if the market goes down, you buy more investments just by accident because you don't change what you're doing. And when the market goes up, those investments are worth more.

For example, if the shares in your 401(k) cost $10/share, and you put in $100 per paycheck, you're buying ten shares. But when the market goes down 50%, and the shares are $5/share, your $100 contribution buys *double* the shares. You now get 20 shares for every $100 contribution.

Now, when the market goes up, you make large gains because you did the smart thing and bought more shares when the market was down (even through you may not have realized it!). So, the accumulation part of getting your qualified money for retirement is not too difficult. It's pretty automatic.

When it's time to live on the money, you begin decumulation. Decumulation requires a paradigm shift in thinking because it's not simply the reverse of putting money in. The rules are entirely different. When you put money in, dollar-cost averaging, it was actually maximizing your investment gains by putting money in every month, even when the market went down.

But when you take money out each month, doing the reverse doesn't work. For example, if you take $1,000/month from your retirement account, and the shares are $100/share, you liquidate ten shares. But if the market tanks 50%, your $1,000 supplement now liquidates 20 shares. Are those shares able to come back with the market? No, they're *gone!* You have accidentally maximized your losses.

And when you take money out, you also have to pay the piper for all the taxes you've deferred. Remember, you received a tax deduction when you put money into your retirement account. Now you must pay taxes on what you put in *plus* taxes on all the growth, when you take money out. The next case study goes more into this.

A MORTGAGE ON YOUR MONEY

Ted came into our office, having retired the week before. He had been to our workshop and wanted to see about a Life Income–Living Asset Cycle℠ plan. He had a million dollars in his IRA and wanted us to show him how to use it for retirement income. Ted was single, which put him in a higher tax bracket than his married friends. This meant that his million dollars was actually worth $650,000 to him after state and federal taxes.

If Ted only took out a little at a time, maybe he wouldn't have to pay that much in taxes. But Ted wanted to pay off his house and his daughter's student loans that he had signed for. That way he could be debt-free in retirement. Well, that came up to a total of over $180,000! With taxes, that $180,000 would cost him $250,000 out of his qualified money.

In addition, Ted needed $7,000 a month to live on. And because of taxes, again, that meant he would have to take out $10,000 a month—$10,000 a month, out of a million, came to 12% a year! What investment is going to support 12% a year? But wait, if he paid off the house and student loan, he would only have $750,000!

Ted didn't understand that he had, essentially, a mortgage on his qualified money. It's actually very similar to a mortgage on a house, but the rules are not as favorable. The mortgage company has a lien against your home. The IRS has a lien against your qualified accounts.

When we get a mortgage on a house, we know exactly how much we owe. Most of the time, we know exactly how much interest we're going to pay. So, if we bought the house for $300,000, with a $200,000 mortgage, and now the house is worth $500,000, does our mortgage change? Well, no.

However, the mortgage on our qualified money does not work on such generous terms. See, you've made a bargain with the IRS. You agreed when you put your money away for retirement that it will be qualified. You will not have to pay taxes on that money before you put it away. But this is a deferral. The money is not tax-free.

When you defer your contributions from taxes, it means you have agreed to pay taxes on all this money later. But, whether you knew it or not, you also agreed to pay taxes on *all* growth later. Remember, if the house goes up in value, you still have the same mortgage. You don't owe more because the value of the house increased. But if your qualified money, your IRA or 401(k), goes up in value, as you hope it will, you actually owe a *larger* mortgage because you have to pay taxes on the growth.

As an example, let's say you have a $500,000 IRA. The market goes up. You now have a $1 million IRA. Well, if your tax rate is 24% federal,

5% state, you owe almost 30% to the government. So, 30% of $500,000 is going to be $150,000.

But if you grow your IRA to $1 million, do you owe $150,000? No. The government now wants $300,000! Your taxes just doubled! And there is another variable you cannot control—tax rates.

This is why tax planning is essential!

PROHIBITED TRANSACTIONS

Donna and Tony bought some real estate with their IRA. Somebody told them that was a great idea. The qualified money would become deferred on the real estate value, and they could grow it without paying taxes or capital gains taxes when they sold the real estate.

But there was a catch nobody told them: if you have an IRA and you own real estate in it, and you do anything to support that property, even something so minor as changing a light bulb, it is no longer an IRA. That is called a prohibited transaction. And now the property is 100% taxable because the IRA has been "broken."

Then we have Justin. He heard on the radio, "You want your IRA in your hands? You don't want to risk it in the market? Buy gold. Put it in your basement." So Justin bought gold, and he put it in his basement. Only one problem. Actually, two.

One, how do you take an RMD out of gold? Do you chip off a piece? I don't think so.

Two, it's considered a prohibited transaction to have custody of your own IRA. You must have a third-party custodian, which means *someone else* has to hold it. You can't hold your own gold. He didn't know that. His IRA was now 100% taxable, and no longer an IRA!

IRS RULES ARE ALWAYS CHANGING

What do all of these case studies we've relayed in this chapter have in common? A lack of knowledge. Without the proper information, you could easily break off that third leg of qualified money from your stool of retirement. The three-legged stool that's supposed to support you throughout retirement could collapse.

Where do you get the information you need? If you have an IRA at Fidelity or a 401(k) at Schwab, that doesn't mean you can call them and get all your answers. They are investment advisors, not decumulation experts. The answers are in the rules and the laws, which change frequently. An investment advisor knows investments, but they may or may not know all of the rules for qualified money.

The only way to rest assured that you'll avoid mistakes is to find an advisor specifically trained in qualified money. We recommend you go to IRAhelp.com to look for one. This is Ed Slott's website. Ed Slott is a CPA (Certified Public Accountant) who specializes in qualified money and testifies in front of Congress about IRA Rules.

Ed has been named "The Best Source for IRA Advice" by *The Wall Street Journal.* As a Master Elite IRA Advisor of Slott's group, Nora goes to all-day classes for three days in a row, twice a year. The new rules added or changed every six months fill a book an inch thick each time. After studying, I must pass an exam to show I know and understand the rules. We spend way too much time correcting mistakes of large institutions whose representatives are not adequately trained.

Because the IRS rules are always changing, we highly recommend you get a qualified advisor for qualified money. If you're set on doing it yourself, then at a minimum you need to be able to coordinate your accounts. You need to make sure you're following the IRS rules and minimizing taxes. But be warned that you won't find any updates to these rules in the newspapers, or on the nightly news.

You can go to www.RetirePluggedIn/bookdownloads to download the RMD factors and percentages both for IRAs and Inherited IRAs, which have very different rules. The rules are there for *before* and *after* the SECURE Act. If you were 70.5 *before* January 1, 2020, you're on the *old* RMD rules. If you made 70.5 *after* January 1, 2020, you're on the *new* RMD rules. If you inherited an IRA *before* January 1, 2020, you're on the *old* Inherited IRA rules. If the IRA owner passed on or after January 1, 2020, you're on the *new* Inherited IRA rules. One more caution: everyone seems to be talking about the SECURE Act, but no one is talking about the IRS *changes* to all the RMD factors in 2021 that started in 2022. Access to updated rules and regulations around qualified money are included in a www.RetirePluggedIn.com membership. When the IRS (or Congress) changes an IRA, 401(k), or similar rule, you'll know immediately so you can avoid additional taxes and penalties!

Also, in the membership site modules are included step-by-step worksheets designed to help you avoid IRA beneficiary and rollover mistakes. Beneficiary mistakes are so prevalent because institutions are *not responsible* if your beneficiaries are not updated, or if they lose them in a computer update. You can also learn about stretch IRA rules, prohibited transactions, and Roth IRA rules, as well as tax planning and much, much more! A membership in www.RetirePluggedIn.com can ensure you avoid mistakes from lack of information, or from reading outdated or incorrect information online.

In the next chapter, we will discuss the risk factors associated with other types of investments.

6

INVESTMENTS

Are You Gambling Away Your Retirement?

"Investments" are defined as committing money to earn a financial return. "Gambling" is the practice of risking loss of something important by taking a chance or betting on a certain outcome. Many of us are putting money into investments as a gamble. We just put the money there and hope that the market will go up rather than down. Which brings us to **Decision #6: How should I invest during retirement?** Take Buddy's story as an example of why gambling doesn't always work out.

Buddy decided to retire in two years, when he turned 66. Then he would get some good Social Security to supplement his qualified money. He already had $700,000 in his 401(k). The year was 2006. He'd been playing it pretty safe, getting ready for retirement. But then he noticed the market suddenly went up 13.62%. He thought, "Whoa, I need to get back in there!"

Buddy moved 100% of his money into the market in 2007. The market only did 3.5% that year. Still, his $700,000 grew to $725,000. So he thought he'd keep it in the market another year. That was unfortunate.

In 2008, the market dropped 55%. Buddy's $724,000 went down to $324,000. Buddy was devastated. He had to delay his retirement until his money could grow back. This took a while.

In 2009, the market went up 23%. It was just over 12% in 2010. In 2011, nothing. No growth. In 2012, the market went up 13.4%. Finally, Buddy got back up to $704,000 in 2014. It took him six years to make back essentially what he'd had before he put all his money in the market. In the process, he lost six years of retirement.

Buddy ended up with a gamble rather than the investment he'd hoped for. You can take a more sophisticated approach. There are tools that allow you to earn an investment return rather than "gambling."

POTS OF MONEY

People often consider investing more of a gamble as they near retirement age. But it is far less so if you make sure you always have three kinds of money, or three pots, to your retirement. This is the basis of our Life Income–Living Asset Cycle℠ plan. Buddy's mistake was that he put all of his money in pot #3, rather than just a portion of it.

Pot #1—Liquid Money ("Now Money")

You need the safe money that's in the bank for emergencies and everyday expenses. We call the money in this first pot "blue money." It's liquid and ready to be used for whatever you need on short notice.

Pot #2—Safe but Growing ("Soon Money")

This money is essentially safe, but it has a better rate of return, or growth. We call this money in pot #2 "green money." It's safe but growing. Everybody needs some liquid money and some safe money that grows more than your liquid money. Usually, this money has a specific reason to be there, such as future guaranteed income, or assistance with paying for long-term care if necessary.

Pot #3—Investments ("Later Money")

Investments make up pot #3. You need investments because risk equals reward. Therefore, you *must* tolerate some risk to get a really good return on your money to have enough for a long life! It's good to have safe money we can rely on for a secure income, but taxes and inflation can be very damaging to your retirement. For you to keep up with inflation and have enough money after taxes, you're probably going to have investments.

But remember, for a bigger reward, you're taking more risk. In fact, sometimes you are taking a *big* risk. A good example is what happened to Buddy's money in 2008. The market went down 55%. We call that a "drawdown." Many people call it a loss. We call it a drawdown because it can come back up. Yet it still took Buddy six years to recover. That meant he was 72 before he got back to where he was to begin with.

Most people don't realize the risk because they've been told that the average rate of return of the market over a good stretch of time is usually 8% to 10%. Many also think the average rate of return works differently than it does. For example, you might think that even in the worst-case scenario, the market goes down 50%, the market goes up 50%, and hey, the average is 0%! I'm okay!

People are often misled by "averages." The "average rate of return" does not equate to the *real* rate of return. You see, using this example, if you have $100,000 and you lose 50%, you have $50,000. Okay. So, the next year you get a 50% return. Do you now have $100,000?

No! Half of $50,000 is $25,000. Therefore, you're now at $75,000! "Average rate of return" of 0% equates to a "real rate of return" of *negative* 25%.

What could Buddy have done differently so he didn't have to wait an additional six years to retire? We'll revisit Buddy's predicament at the end of the chapter.

WRONG PLACE, RIGHT TIME

The average rate of return also doesn't mean a lot if you're in the wrong place at the right time. Take as an example, Daniel and Dave, two brothers who retired with the same amount in their retirement accounts. They also drew out the same amount of money. But they had vastly different results because of a little-known danger called "sequence of returns risk."

Daniel had a large 401(k) with $1 million in it. Between 2000 and 2014, there were many ups and downs in the market. Daniel began the year 2000 with three losses. By 2014, he would have just had three years of gains. Even if we swapped places with his gains and losses, though, he would have had the exact same "returns."

Daniel understood that, which is why he wasn't worried. He understood the "commutative property of multiplication." Put in simple terms: 2 × 3 = 6, and if you reverse that order, 3 × 2, the answer is still 6. If you look at the chart below, you'll see that those gains could have been in the beginning and the losses at the end, and his returns would have been exactly the same.

In other words, the "sequence of returns," the ups and downs in the market and what sequence they were in, would not have mattered at all, *if he had not retired and started withdrawing!*

Sequence of Returns During *Accumulation Phase*

Year	Historical Return of S&P 500 Annual Return	Withdrawal (G)	Basis Withdrawal (G) / Withdrawal (N)	$1,000,000 / End of Year Value	Inflation / Inverse Return	2.5% / Withdrawal (N)	Tax (Fed & State) 20.00% / End of Year Value
2000	-10.10%	$0	$0	$899,000	11.39%	$0	$1,113,900
2001	-13.00%	$0	$0	$782,130	29.60%	$0	$1,443,614
2002	-23.40%	$0	$0	$599,112	13.41%	$0	$1,637,203
2003	26.40%	$0	$0	$757,277	0.00%	$0	$1,637,203
2004	9.00%	$0	$0	$825,432	12.80%	$0	$1,846,765
2005	3.00%	$0	$0	$850,195	23.50%	$0	$2,280,755
2006	13.62%	$0	$0	$965,991	-38.50%	$0	$1,402,664
2007	3.53%	$0	$0	$1,000,091	3.53%	$0	$1,452,178
2008	-38.50%	$0	$0	$615,056	13.62%	$0	$1,649,965
2009	23.50%	$0	$0	$759,594	3.00%	$0	$1,699,464
2010	12.80%	$0	$0	$856,822	9.00%	$0	$1,852,416
2011	0.00%	$0	$0	$856,822	26.40%	$0	$2,341,453
2012	13.41%	$0	$0	$971,722	-23.40%	$0	$1,793,553
2013	29.60%	$0	$0	$1,259,352	-13.00%	$0	$1,560,391
2014	11.39%	$0	$0	$1,402,792	-10.10%	$0	$1,402,792

Annual Returns have been pre-populated based on total return of the S&P500 index using a calendar year 1/1 - 12/31 as points of reference for calculation

The negative returns in pink are exactly the same, just in inverse order. Therefore, as seen in the boxes at the bottom of the chart, the returns and result were the same! Daniel retired in the year 2000. His brother, Dave, had successfully retired earlier. Dave took out $60,000 a year, and he never ran out of money,

Daniel thought, "If it worked for Dave, it should work for me!" Daniel decided to follow his brother's success. However, in the year 2000, when Daniel retired, we had three market losses in a row, 10%, 13%, and 23%, the inverse of what Dave had experienced. Daniel continued to take out $60,000 a year just as Dave had done, but Daniel ran out of money in 2011! What happened to the "commutative property of multiplication"? Why did this strategy work for one brother but not the other? We'll revisit this case study later in the chapter to understand.

A PARADIGM SHIFT IN INVESTING

Thinking about retirement requires a total paradigm shift because what got you here won't get you there! What you did to get where you are when you're ready to retire won't work as well *after* retirement. You see, most of us accumulate money in our 401(k)s and IRAs by putting money in monthly. All most people know is that no matter what, whether the market goes up or the market goes down, we should put that money in every month.

Like we discussed in the previous chapter, this strategy of accumulating money is called "dollar-cost averaging." If the market is up and we put in $100 a month, we can purchase ten shares for $10 each, for example. That's good. But when the market drops while we're accumulating, it's even better.

If the market drops 50%, for example, then the share value we're purchasing is $5 a share instead of $10. So now we get 20 shares for the same $100 we put in. When the market goes up, those shares grow. We have just maximized our investment!

This is where the paradigm shift for retirement comes in. Because, when you're accumulating, you're automatically buying more shares when the market goes down. And you don't care as much if it's down, because you have time on your side.

But when you quit working, you're "decumulating" or going into the "distribution phase" rather than the "accumulation phase." Losses matter when you have to liquidate shares to live on. You will not gain those losses back because the shares are no longer there!

And if you remember the last chapter, you also have to account for taxes. If you don't know how to make your money last through decumulation, or the "distribution phase," it could be disastrous!

Buy and Hope

A theory of investments that we see and hear everywhere is that people should buy investments and hold them, "buy and hold." We hear, "You'd be stupid to get out of the market when the market goes down. This would just confirm and guarantee a loss." Well, that sounds like it makes sense, and when you're accumulating it does. When you're accumulating, this strategy works!

However, when you're decumulating and you "buy and hold," we like to call it "buy and *hope*." You risk liquidating your investments. You see, the rules are different if you dollar-cost average *out*. This means taking out the same amount every month to live on, just like you put the same amount every month in to accumulate. You might think it would work the same, but it won't.

When you dollar-cost average *in*, you maximize your gains. When those low share values go up, you make money. When you dollar-cost average *out*, what might be the problem?

Let's look at Bruce as an example. Bruce needs $2,000 a month extra to live on during retirement. If he took out $2,000/month and his shares were $100 a share, he would liquidate 20 shares each month.

Now, those 20 shares are gone, but the others can continue to grow. However, if the market goes down, the shares are not worth $100 anymore. Let's say the shares are now worth $50 each. How many shares does Bruce have to liquidate to get his $2,000?

That's right. Bruce now has to liquidate *40* shares that will never have a chance to grow back. But this isn't Bruce's only problem.

Bruce's other problem is that "sequence of returns" risk. What does that mean? Returns are the returns you expect to earn on your money in the market. The sequence is the order of those returns. For instance, there might be years when the market goes up. Those are gains. When the market goes down, those are losses.

Does it matter what order they happen in? Well, if you're accumulating it doesn't matter because of the "commutative property of multiplication," as we mentioned earlier. If you multiply two numbers, it doesn't matter what order they're in: 6 × 7 or 7 × 6 both equal 42. However, when we start withdrawing our funds, now it makes a difference. We'll return to Dave and Daniel to get a better understanding of why we need that paradigm shift.

SEQUENCE OF RETURNS

What happened to Daniel's retirement? Well, his older brother, Dave, had retired earlier. He had the same returns, but he had three gaining years first. He went through the down period later. He did not run out of money. This is because sequence of returns matters when you're decumulating, or are in the "distribution phase." It determines whether you get rich or run out of money.

Let's look at what happened to Daniel when he relied on the "average return" while withdrawing versus Dave who had the same returns, but in the inverse order. The chart below shows both withdrawing $60,000 a year with a 2.5% inflation factor to keep up with increasing costs in retirement.

Daniel's and Dave's Annual Withdrawals, with Inflation

				Daniel			Dave
	Historical Return		Basis	$1,000,000	Inflation	2.5%	Tax (Fed & State) 20.00%
Year	of S&P 500		Withdrawal (G)	$60,000			
	Annual Return	Withdrawal (G)	Withdrawal (N)	End of Year Value	Inverse Return	Withdrawal (N)	End of Year Value
2000	-10.10%	$60,000	$48,000	$839,000	11.39%	$48,000	$1,053,900
2001	-13.00%	$61,500	$49,200	$668,430	29.60%	$49,200	$1,304,354
2002	-23.40%	$63,038	$50,430	$448,980	13.41%	$50,430	$1,416,231
2003	26.40%	$64,613	$51,691	$502,897	0.00%	$51,691	$1,351,617
2004	9.00%	$66,229	$52,983	$481,929	12.80%	$52,983	$1,458,396
2005	3.00%	$67,884	$54,308	$428,502	23.50%	$54,308	$1,733,234
2006	13.62%	$69,582	$55,665	$417,283	-38.50%	$55,665	$996,357
2007	3.53%	$71,321	$57,057	$360,692	3.53%	$57,057	$960,208
2008	-38.50%	$73,104	$58,483	$148,721	13.62%	$58,483	$1,017,884
2009	23.50%	$74,932	$59,945	$108,739	3.00%	$59,945	$973,488
2010	12.80%	$76,805	$61,444	$45,853	9.00%	$61,444	$984,297
2011	0.00%	$78,725	$62,980	($32,873)	26.40%	$62,980	$1,165,427
2012	13.41%	$80,693	$64,555	($117,974)	-23.40%	$64,555	$812,024
2013	29.60%	$82,711	$66,169	($235,605)	-13.00%	$66,169	$623,750
2014	11.39%	$84,778	$67,823	($347,219)	-10.10%	$67,823	$475,973

Annual Returns have been pre-populated based on total return of the S&P500 index using a calendar year 1/1 - 12/31 as points of reference for calculation

Daniel just happened to retire when the market had three years of losses. How can you predict that? You can't! So, what can you do? You must leave behind the old thinking.

We've all been taught "asset allocation" and "buy and hold." Asset allocation feels like we're being careful, "Don't put all your eggs in one basket." Put your investments into *both* "equities and fixed income." To translate, split between stocks and bonds. In fact, we've probably also been told to put more into bonds as we get older and less into stocks, because "bonds are less risky."

If stocks go up, usually bonds go down. And if bonds go down, stocks go up. This is the theory. We hope that we'll balance out. The problem is that, at any given time, the market may go up or down. We just don't know!

Bonds, however, have a correlation to interest rates. If you look at the seesaw below, you'll see that if interest rates go up, bond values go down. If bond values go up, interest rates go down.

Bonds & Interest Rates

Market Interest Rates and Prices of Fixed-Rate Bonds
Move in Opposite Directions

Interest Rates and Bond Prices Move in Opposite Directions

Source: SEC Pub. No. 151 issued 6/13.

Lower Market Interest Rates → Higher Fixed-Rate Bond Prices
Higher Market Interest Rates → Lower Fixed-Rate Bond Prices

Interest rates are still at some of the lowest they have ever been in over 50 years. This means that they are most likely to go up. And when interest rates go up, bond values go down. Both equities (stocks) and fixed income (bonds) are risky. So, what can we do to avoid the large drawdowns, or losses?

One strategy that can help is called "tactical management." You can think of it like taking a GPS on your road trip.

TACTICAL MANAGEMENT

Most of us these days have a GPS. If we don't, and we run into a traffic jam, we don't know how long we're going to sit there. We don't know how much time we're going to lose. It could be stop and go for five minutes. It could be hours.

How long is it going to take us to make up that lost time, not to mention the serious kink in our travel plans? Similarly, if we "buy and hold" in our investment accounts, we don't know how much we're going lose. Nor do we know how long it's going to take us to make up the loss. It can cost us a lot of time we can't get back.

But tactical management is like having a GPS when we're in traffic. We reach a traffic jam, and our GPS says, "Auto re-direct. Take the next exit." Or "Traffic jam ahead. Finding new route."

Our GPS may move us forward slowly, but it's always working to move us forward. It keeps us moving at a steady and safe rate along the new route, instead of being at risk of losing a large amount of time and money. We may even get special indicators and warnings that allow us to avoid the traffic jam, or losses, altogether.

Mutual Funds

So, is tactical management essentially a mutual fund that manages your investments? Absolutely not! Unfortunately, mutual funds are required by law to file an "objective" with the Securities and Exchange Commission

(SEC). If they say "I'm a large cap mutual fund (stocks with market capitalization of $10 billion or more)," then they must be invested at least 85% in large cap stocks, no matter what the market does.

With a mutual fund, if large cap stocks are all losing value, your account manager can't just change your investment to small cap stocks. He can pick the best stocks for his filed objective, another large cap stock, but he can't pick when to get in and out of the market. He *must* keep you invested!

Tactical management is not "timing the market." No one has successfully ever done that, because it's based on someone's feeling or emotions. Tactical management uses mathematical algorithms to tell the manager when, historically, the market may continue to go down, or up, and therefore give the manager a chance to move you out of harm's way. And mutual funds alone cannot do that.

Separately Managed Accounts

Tactical management is offered through a vehicle called a separately managed account (SMA). Investopedia defines "managed separate accounts" as "a portfolio of assets managed by a professional investment firm" such as a "registered investment advisor." They go on to say, "SMAs differ from pooled vehicles like mutual funds in that each portfolio is unique."

SMAs were rarely offered to the "retail" sector (that's you and me!) until 2008, when ordinary people in the investment world started figuring out that "buy and hold" doesn't work. We now can take advantage of the same type of management that institutional investors with over $25 million have had access to for decades.

There are still a lot of investment advisors out there who tell their personal clients, "Asset allocate. Buy and hold." Usually that's because they don't have access to SMAs or don't understand them. But because of the experience many investors had in 2008, they're seeking out advisors who have access to this new (to us!) way of investing.

WHAT GOT YOU HERE WON'T GET YOU THERE

Moving into retirement requires a paradigm shift in your thinking about investments. As the example of Daniel and his brother, Dave, shows, decumulation is not simply the reverse of the accumulation you do while investing for retirement. Sequence of returns matter when you're decumulating.

While Buddy had a great "asset allocated" portfolio of stocks and bonds, that didn't protect him. It all went down in 2008! He could have benefited from tactical management. He would definitely have benefited from an independent advisor. He and Daniel both!

This chapter focused on pot #3: investments. But it's important to have money in all three pots. In the next chapter, we will discuss the importance of pot #2: green, growing, safe money.

7

GUARANTEED INCOME

Is Your Income Guaranteed for Life?

In the previous chapter, we recommended that you have three pots of money when you retire. These pots form the basis of our Life Income–Living Asset Cycle^{SM} plan. The last chapter was all about pot #3: investments. In this chapter, we look at how you can use certain tools to make a guaranteed income that will last. We will show you how to create this income with pot #2: safety, with decent growth. This will be **Decision #7: How much guaranteed income do I need, and how do I get it?**

With a guaranteed income, we also have to think about inflation down the road, as well the potential cost of long-term care. You may have enough money now, but you need to have a supplemental guaranteed income that grows over time, so you can continue to live as comfortably as you are today.

Statistically, most of us are going to live 20 to 30 years in retirement, according to the Social Security Administration's 2007 Period Life Table. If you're married, one of you has a 50% chance of living to age 95, and one or both may need long-term care. These are things you need to plan for.

Most of us have some income that we believe should be for life. We have Social Security, maybe a pension. You've probably put together an IRA or contribute to a 401(k), a TSP, or a 403(b). Yet how do you know if this is enough?

If you need $5,000/month today to live comfortably, you're probably going to need closer to $10,000/month in 25 years. Why? Historically inflation has averaged 2.8% to 3%. That *doubles* the income needed to maintain exactly the same standard of living!

So, what do you do if your cost-of-living increases on your pension or Social Security aren't keeping up with inflation? What if you need additional money for long-term care? How do you create additional income?

In Gary and Mary's case, the two had been married forever, it seemed. They never thought too much about long-term care because they would take care of each other. Even so, Gary didn't want to burden Mary, so he purchased long-term care insurance for himself from his employer, the federal government.

Gary knew Mary probably couldn't lift him, for example, since he was a big man. But Gary could take care of Mary if anything happened, and they didn't want the added expense of another premium. Then Mary's mother got Alzheimer's disease.

Mary's mother lived with Alzheimer's for ten years. Mary was able to care for her at home the first five years, until even with outside help, she couldn't handle Mom at home anymore. Mary's mother was in facility care over five more years.

The cost of care over those five years was astronomical. Now, planning for long-term care for Mary became quite real. Since Alzheimer's seemed to run in families, it became a real concern for both Gary and Mary.

Gary was scared enough that he went to the federal government, his previous employer. He asked them about adding Mary to his long-term care group plan. But because Mary had preexisting conditions, the federal government turned her down.

Mary's health problems weren't that serious—arthritis, the antidepressants she took while caring for her mother, and a couple of small skin cancers that had been removed. But this was all it took to get denied. Mary got turned down by not just the federal government but by every independent company they applied to.

Gary was most worried about long-term care, but he also worried about inflation. He knew he and Mary were going to need more income. They didn't need it now, but they would need it in the future. What could he and Mary do?

Working in Gary and Mary's favor was the fact that creating an income in the future is much easier than creating an income today because the money has time to grow. We'll revisit the options available to them later in this chapter.

THE THREE-LEGGED STOOL OF RETIREMENT

We've talked about the three legs necessary to keep the retirement stool of income balanced. The three legs are your pension, Social Security, and your own savings, which is usually a 401(k), an IRA, or another such retirement account.

Leg #1: Pensions

A pension is one leg of the stool. If you only have a pension to live on, then you have a one-legged stool. Don't get me wrong. Pensions are wonderful! A pension can be an income for life. The only problem is that if the company runs out of money, your pension can be reduced. You're very fortunate if you've worked for the federal government, because they can just print some money if they run out!

Leg #2: Social Security

Social Security is a second leg on that stool. Many of us have heard that Social Security is going to run out of money. However, as mentioned before, it's not going to run out of money if you're approaching retirement now. It may not pay as much as you hope, but it should be there the rest of your life. If you have Social Security but no pension, then you have a one-legged stool.

Leg #3: Qualified Money—Your IRA or 401(k)

The third leg isn't turned into income as readily. So how do we turn that third leg into income? First of all, we have to have money available to do it. Usually, these funds are from a retirement account you've built, but there are other types of accounts, as well. Maybe you put money away from an inheritance when your parents or grandparents passed away. Or maybe you've been slowly putting money in the bank for years. Now you have a lump sum that you want to turn into a guaranteed income in the future.

Another Source of Income

Another source of income that can stand in for one of these legs is home equity. Many of us have lived in our homes for a very long time. We have likely paid off our home, or almost paid it off by retirement, and there is equity there.

Is it possible to turn that home equity into an income stream? It is. A **home equity conversion mortgage**, or HECM, is also known as a "reverse mortgage." While this program used to be cost prohibitive for many people, the federal government has since changed the laws to make it more consumer friendly.

PAUL AND SHIRLEY'S REVERSE MORTGAGE

Now, we are not big fans of reverse mortgages in most situations. But, as I've mentioned before in this book, it depends. Everyone's situation is different. So, let's take a look at Paul and Shirley's situation.

Paul and Shirley had been very frugal their entire lives. Unfortunately, they had no pension. They had Social Security but found that the included cost-of-living increases weren't enough. The Medicare premium kept rising to keep pace with the Social Security increase until Paul and Shirley could no longer live comfortably. What could they do?

Paul and Shirley's home was paid for, and they had a lot of equity in it. They knew that if they took out a loan on the equity, then they would have a mortgage. Paying that would be difficult. They'd heard of a reverse mortgage. But mostly they'd heard horror stories.

Paul and Shirley had heard that when you died, the mortgage company took your house. Your kids got nothing. This scared Paul and Shirley. They'd also heard that the mortgage company could just decide, "Hey, I'm going to call this mortgage and take your house." This scared them even more.

Well, neither of those stories about reverse mortgages are true. The truth is that you simply have a mortgage that will have to be paid off at some time in the future. But the payment is not due until you either leave the house or you die. When you die, your kids will still inherit the house. But they will have to pay off the mortgage, which is something to consider.

Sounds Great! How Do I Turn a Reverse Mortgage into Income?

You have to be at least 62 years old to qualify for an HECM. You do not need to qualify by income, but you need enough equity in the house to take a loan against it. You also have to pay your insurance and taxes on the house every year. And the house must be in decent shape. Then, you can choose from one of three following options, or even divide your equity between two or three options.

Option #1: Take a lump sum.

Option #2: Take an income stream.

Option #3: Have a line of credit.

Why would you choose one of these options over another? Why not just take your money now, instead of taking an income stream? Or why take an equity line of credit instead of a lump sum?

Well, you wouldn't want to take out a lump sum unless it was necessary. With a lump sum, interest can build up and actually take away the remaining equity. You should only take out what you need.

Now, if you get an equity line of credit but you don't use it, you actually get interest credited to your account. So, it grows your line of credit. If you think you ***might*** need a lump sum later, don't take it out now. Get your line of credit, and let it grow.

Since Paul and Shirley really needed a guaranteed income, they took a portion of their reverse mortgage as a guaranteed income for life for both of them. But what would happen if an emergency came up and they needed a little more money? Thinking about this, they also took part of the house's value as a home equity line of credit. They actually took a part of option #2 and a part of option #3.

Unlike a regular mortgage, there are no payments due immediately with a reverse mortgage. In fact, payment is only due when you die or both owners (if you're married) leave the house permanently or sell it. Just like when you take out a regular loan, each disbursement of money that you get has an interest rate on it. The interest grows inside of the mortgage. You don't pay it. That's the good news. It's also the bad news.

But the growing interest is only really bad news if you have kids who want the house. And it's only bad news for them. This is because that interest rate that you aren't paying is compounding what is owed. Even that, however, is not really bad news, because the mortgage company can never collect more than the house is worth, even if you owe hundreds of thousands more over time!

Now, Paul and Shirley had no children, so it didn't matter to them. If you do have children, any equity left in the house will still go to them once the mortgage is taken care of. If not your children, someone's going to get that equity when you die! It's a myth that the mortgage company will take the house with all the remaining equity.

For Paul and Shirley, the reverse mortgage was an excellent solution to getting guaranteed income. But keep in mind that there are other options besides taking money out of your house. CD laddering is another strategy for generating income. You could even buy CDs (Certificates of Deposit) with the equity from your home.

CD LADDERING

Sometimes people want a safer income from the equity in their homes. Nora's parents were an example of this. When they retired, they laddered CDs. They took money from selling rental property, and they got a CD at the bank that had a high interest rate.

They took out a CD now, three months from now, and six months from now. This is called "laddering." Why would they do that? Because income is generated from the CDs, and one CD matures every three months, freeing up a lump sum if they needed it.

How CDs Work

To get a CD, you basically give the bank a lump sum in return for a promise that you're going to let that lump sum sit there and gain interest. (Meanwhile, they're using your money to make more than they're giving you!) The bank usually promises a particular amount of interest on the front side. That interest compounds while your money sits there. But the deal is that you have to let the money sit there for the promised amount of time.

Let's say that you have a two-year CD. If something comes up and you need that money after six months, you are going to have to pay back six months of interest. What if you don't have six months of interest because the money has been in the CD only three months so far?

The bank doesn't care! You will have to pay them six months of interest, regardless, if you want that lump sum back. So, locking up money can be a problem. But many people like CDs because they guarantee interest. They know they're going to get interest, and there's no market risk.

There is a downside to CDs, though. Let's say you're getting 1.5% interest on a two-year CD and you're in a 25% tax bracket. That interest is taxed at your current tax rate once you receive it. If you're in a 25% federal tax bracket and a 5% state tax bracket, you have just lost 30% of your 1.5% profit. Inflation can also be a problem.

For my parents, CD laddering worked well for some time. They retired in 1980, when CD rates were 14.28%! This strategy doesn't work as well if the interest rate is low, of course. I still have one of their CD certificates, pictured below.

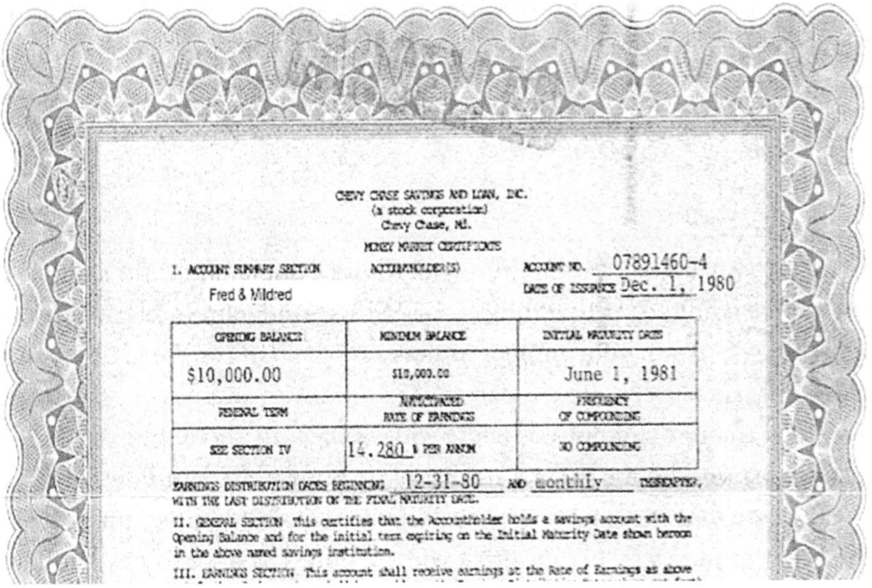

CHEVY CHASE SAVINGS AND LOAN, INC.
(a stock corporation)
Chevy Chase, Md.

MONEY MARKET CERTIFICATES

I. ACCOUNT SUMMARY SECTION — ACCOUNTHOLDER(S) — ACCOUNT NO. 07891460-4

Fred & Mildred — DATE OF ISSUANCE Dec. 1, 1980

OPENING BALANCE	MINIMUM BALANCE	INITIAL MATURITY DATE
$10,000.00	$10,000.00	June 1, 1981
RENEWAL TERM	ANTICIPATED RATE OF EARNINGS	FREQUENCY OF COMPOUNDING
SEE SECTION IV	14.280 % PER ANNUM	NO COMPOUNDING

EARNINGS DISTRIBUTION DATES BEGINNING 12-31-80 AND monthly THEREAFTER, WITH THE LAST DISTRIBUTION ON THE FINAL MATURITY DATE.

II. GENERAL SECTION This certifies that the Accountholder holds a savings account with the Opening Balance and for the initial term expiring on the Initial Maturity Date shown hereon in the above named savings institution.

III. EARNINGS SECTION This account shall receive earnings at the Rate of Earnings as above

CD Money Market Certificate from 1980

My parents were hard-working folks who didn't have pensions. They both had Social Security but knew that would not be enough. My dad had a well-thought-out plan for retirement. He would buy a house, we'd live in it for a time, then we'd move. He'd rent the house out and let the rent pay the mortgage. He would then sell the houses when he retired and put the money in CDs so they could live off the interest.

This is what my parents did. And they were earning over $1,000/ month on their $100,000. Meanwhile, I had graduated from college and was earning less than that teaching school full-time! Most think of CDs as "stable," but the chart below shows the volatility of CD rates.

Historic CD Interest Rates (1984–2021)

Source: https://www.bankrate.com/banking/cds/historical-cd-interest-rates/

The risk with CDs is that inflation could be more than what you earn *net*. If it is, inflation eats up your principal needed to stay on top of payments for everything else. For my parents, it was difficult near the end. CD rates dropped and inflation went up, so they had to dip into their principal.

When my parents passed, there was only $30,000 left. They had guaranteed income from the CDs, but no guarantee of how much interest they would generate. My parents' story shows why you need more ways to generate income that can be guaranteed for life.

As we've said before, most people retire because they can. In other words, they have enough income, or they think they do. However, there is often a need for additional guaranteed income in many situations, such as with Jack and Linda in the next section.

REVERSIONARY ANNUITY FOR SURVIVOR BENEFIT

Jack and Linda retired very comfortably. However, Jack had not taken a survivorship benefit for his wife on his pension, just like Ed in the Overview. That survivorship benefit costs money. He thought they could better use that money to live on.

This meant that if Jack died first, Linda wasn't going to get even half his pension. Linda also was going to lose one of their Social Security checks. In short, Linda was going to have a real problem. Jack realized that he messed up here. But they wouldn't let him go back and take that survivor benefit. What else could he do?

Well, what Jack learned is that for the same 10% of his retirement that he would've paid for the survivor benefit, he could get another tool called the Reversionary Annuity. With a Reversionary Annuity Jack would pay every month, just like he would for the survivor's benefit. The Reversionary Annuity even had an advantage the survivor benefit didn't.

First of all, if Jack paid into the Reversionary Annuity every month and he passed away, the Reversionary Annuity guaranteed Linda an income for the rest of her life. This part worked just like a survivor benefit. However, he also chose a rider—if Linda predeceased him, unlike with the survivor benefit, he would get all his money back.

Now, the return of premium disbursements would be scheduled over ten years, but he would get all of his premiums back if he lived that long. If not, the company would keep the difference, which wouldn't matter if Linda had already passed. Whichever of them passed first, the survivor would have an increase in income! Survivor benefits don't do that.

In addition, the Reversionary Annuity has a tax advantage. A survivor benefit gives you income that is 100% state and federally taxable. However, with the Reversionary Annuity—because it is an annuity, which we're going to talk about shortly—only about 15% of the amount is taxable. If Linda got $3,000 a month, she would pay taxes on less than $1,000 of that.

The saved taxes made this better than the survivor's benefit Jack could have gotten through his pension because it increased Linda's net spendable income. Jack was fortunate that he was healthy. Otherwise, he would not have qualified for this tool.

Many of our clients have this tool; however, as of this writing, it is not available! Then why would I bring it up and explain it? Two reasons: (1) If and when it becomes available again, it's an awesome tool! (2) To illustrate a *very important fact*—if you find a tool that fits your needs, don't procrastinate too long because it could be gone tomorrow! These products change often, and good ones that are available today could be taken off the market (without warning!) before you can get them. In this industry, "you snooze, you lose!"

GARY AND MARY LEARN ABOUT ANNUITIES

If you remember Gary and Mary from the beginning of the chapter, they continued their search for long-term care by looking into annuities. Gary already had a pension from the federal government. That was also called an annuity. Gary thought that was what an annuity was: getting income for life starting now.

In reality, a pension is actually what we technically call an "annuitization." This means that Gary had a lump sum of money with the government, and they were providing him an income stream from it.

Gary knew that if he passed away, his wife lost part of that income stream. If they both passed away, nobody got the money. When he heard the word "annuity," this was what he thought of.

However, an annuity is *not* an income stream; it's simply a lump sum of money, similar to a savings or investment account. That money sits in an insurance contract that keeps the earnings tax deferred until distribution. But it's also *not* an IRA!

As Gary was soon to learn, you have choices with an annuity. You don't have to annuitize like his pension. But you can. And if he annuitized—and this is what scared him—would he have to give them all of his money to have an income stream?

Sure, it would provide an income stream guaranteed for life, but he was worried. What about their kids? If he and Mary were both gone, would the company just keep the money?

There is something called a Single Premium Immediate Annuity, known as a SPIA, which is exactly that. You give up your money, and in return you get an income stream for life. But if you die, nobody gets it. For those who don't have any children, this might be a decent option.

But what Gary and Mary wanted was an income stream with something left over for their kids if they both died. Luckily, there are many different types of annuities to choose from. They could get an annuity providing income for life with a period certain, meaning it would last as long as they did, but if they died early, it would continue to pay their heirs for that certain period they chose.

For example, Gary and Mary could get an annuity that would pay for both their lives, with a minimum of 10 or 20 years, whichever they chose. Yet if they both died tomorrow, their children would get the income for the remainder of the 10 or 20 years. For them, this last one seemed the best, particularly because they wanted to be sure that this income would be there in case Mary ended up with Alzheimer's like her mother.

Variable Annuities

Gary and Mary discovered that there are many kinds of annuities. There is an SPIA, as we've mentioned, which gives you guaranteed income for the rest of your life, with a period certain or without. There are also Variable Annuities. Gary had heard that a Variable Annuity had investments in it, and he was used to having investments in his IRA, so the Variable Annuity initially appealed to Gary.

What Gary didn't know was that the Variable Annuity gives no guarantees of income for life unless you pay for a rider. It also doesn't guarantee you won't lose all of your money in the market. Worse yet, there are high fees on it, even without a rider, because of something called mortality and expense charges, or "M&E" fees, in addition to other fees. Total fees start at about 3% and, for many of them, go up to 5%.

The M&E charges are necessary because Variable Annuities do have one important guarantee. You can lose all your money in the market, but if you hold it until you die, your heirs will get what dollars you put in, minus any withdrawals, when you die. Gary was concerned about leaving something for his kids but more concerned about Mary's income if he predeceased her. This wasn't the annuity for them.

Fixed Annuities

A fixed annuity is like a CD, yet a little different. Difference number one: you generally get a higher interest rate. Difference number two: there's no 1099 tax form sent to you at the end of the year to file. Due to a rule of the IRS, you do not have to pay taxes on the interest you earn inside the annuity until you decide to take the money out. Therefore, you decide when to pay the taxes!

"Fixed" means the principal is guaranteed. You can't lose it. Although fixed annuities pay a bit more than CDs, Gary wasn't sure they could generate enough income for him and Mary. He wasn't sure how to make this work so that their children got money if they died.

Fixed Index Annuities

Now, fixed, as we've said, means you can't lose your principal. Most of us have heard of the S&P index or the Nasdaq index. In fact, the fixed index annuity actually ties your interest to an index such as these. If the market goes up, your account goes up. If the market goes down, you are guaranteed not to lose your principal because it is a fixed index annuity.

The fixed index annuity appealed to Gary. However, Gary knew if it sounded too good to be true, it probably was. The catch is that, while a fixed index annuity does go up with the market, there are caps. This means that if the market goes up 10%, maybe you only get 4% of that gain.

There are also other strategies within the fixed index annuity game. Some of them say you can have a "participation rate." That means you "participate" to a certain percentage. If you have 80% participation and the market goes up 10%, you get 8%.

The one thing Gary knew for sure was that he needed to learn more about the mechanics and the rules. The ins and outs seemed complicated. Gary feared he could be easily misled by a salesperson. Gary contacted an advisor after he and Mary did their initial research. From the advisor, Gary learned which annuities might work best for them.

Added Guaranteed Income for Life Rider

Gary and Mary's advisor explained that many of these fixed index annuities can add an "income for life" rider. Some had a fee of 1% or less, but some were free! This rider would mean that not only is Gary's money safe from being lost in the market, but it could possibly grow more than in the bank. Gary could also set it up so he could turn this income on for himself and Mary in the future.

This income would be guaranteed for both their lives, and they wouldn't have to give up their principal. They could actually get any remaining principal after taking withdrawals, if they wanted. And when they died, their heirs would get what was left.

Some of these guaranteed income riders actually double the income if you or your spouse needs long-term care. If you remember from Chapter 4, the federal qualification for long-term care is the loss of two of six "activities of daily living." Those activities are bathing, eating, dressing, continence, toileting, and transferring. If Gary or Mary were to lose the ability to complete two of these six activities of daily living on their own, they not only get the income that they may have already turned on, but it doubles for up to five years. The income then continues after the five years, but at the original rate.

A traditional long-term-care policy is usually "reimbursement" based, meaning you pay the bills, then submit them to the insurance company. If approved, the insurance company pays you. To be approved, you usually must use professional services, or be in a qualified facility. You can't pay a family member or neighbor to come in and help.

With this income from the riders, you don't have to get reimbursed. The money goes directly into your bank account, and you can spend it any way you want! You can even save or invest it if you don't need all of it. Then, after five years, the income drops down to the amount you were originally receiving and continues for both your lives.

The good news was that Mary didn't have to qualify if Gary owned this annuity for two years and she was not in need of care at the time that they bought it! Not only would they be guaranteed the income for life when they turned it on, the money could double for up to five years, which was exactly how long Mary's mother needed care for Alzheimer's.

Life Insurance

Life insurance is another option people don't often consider for income. There are now policies called Indexed Universal Life (IUL), where you can contribute a lump sum, or you can buy it over time. Meanwhile, that money sits there to grow. When you need money, you can pull it out tax-free.

Gary learned that you can buy a policy, even if you don't qualify, as Mary wouldn't. You can buy a policy on someone else for the benefit of yourself. Well, hold the train. How does that work?

Life insurance has three parts to it: the owner, the insured, and the beneficiary. They can be three different people. Gary needed money for Mary, but she wouldn't qualify. He could actually have her be the owner of a policy for himself. He could be the insured because he did qualify, and they could both be beneficiaries for the income.

Another solution! But which one was best? Gary went through all of the numbers with his advisor. What he learned here was that since all of the money they would take out on the life insurance was technically a loan, they would not have to pay taxes.

That was a big benefit! For comparison, if you need $3,500 a month and take that money out of the growth on an annuity, or an IRA, you will probably have to take out $5,000 to account for taxes. This will liquidate the account faster than if you can just take out $3,500 tax-free.

By seeking the help of a knowledgeable advisor, Gary and Mary were finally able to find some answers to their long-term care coverage dilemma.

FIND A KNOWLEDGEABLE ADVISOR

Especially if you run into problems making your money last in retirement, it's in your best interest to find a knowledgeable advisor. Jack was relieved to solve the problem of a survivor benefit for Linda with the Reversionary Annuity, but this tool may not work for everyone.

With the help of an advisor, you too can find the best solution for your circumstances. Maybe you're set with your pension, Social Security, and an IRA. Maybe you plan to take a reverse mortgage as a backup plan. Maybe you can take out some equity to do CD ladders. Maybe an annuity, or even life insurance, can provide the future income you need to account for inflation, long-term care, or anything else.

There are more possibilities than what we've included in this chapter. And what might work best for you depends on your situation. "It depends," as we like to say. This is why we recommend getting an advisor. But if you're a committed do-it-yourselfer, you can find more information at our www.RetirePluggedIn.com/bookdownloads website. There you can download a free white paper, "Guaranteed Income."

If you think determining a guaranteed income for the next 20 to 30 years is complicated, just wait until we get to taxes in the next chapter. You can't adequately plan for retirement unless you've really sat down and figured out how taxes will affect your income. Because they will.

8

TAXES

The Biggest Bombshell

Ah, retirement at last! Michelle and Monty had worked hard and saved a long time. Monty was really looking forward to not having to commute anymore. They imagined evenings of being well rested enough to actually talk to each other. They would spend weekends doing things other than catching up on housework. They could go see their grandchildren when they wanted. And they would have time to help Michelle's ailing parents, something that weighed heavy on their minds. Maybe they could even resurrect some hobbies.

Although they had worked very hard, Michelle and Monty were afraid. What if there wasn't enough money to enjoy themselves? What if they had to help Michelle's parents financially? They wanted to be able to enjoy their freedom. They wanted to travel and do things, but what if all they had saved was not enough?

It turned out that Michelle and Monty were right to be worried. While their planning looked good up front, they had not made a tax-efficient plan. They needed to make **Decision #8: How do I use my savings tax-efficiently to increase net income?**

When Michelle and Monty came to see us, they had not only saved every bit they could but they had also put together an expense sheet. This is something we always tell our clients to do, and they had already done it! They knew what their preretirement expenses were: about $10,000 a month. They also knew that, once they retired, their expenses would go down to about $8,000 a month. They had already done this legwork.

With all their savings, a pension, and Social Security, Michelle and Monty hoped they would be okay. But they wanted us to check it out. And it turned out to be a good thing for them that they did.

THREE FAULTY ASSUMPTIONS

Michelle had stayed at home raising the kids, but Monty had worked 30 years with the same company and would receive a pension of $1,200 a month. He knew that money was going to be there. His Social Security at age 66 would be $2,600/month, and Michelle could collect half of it, $1,300/month.

Their total guaranteed income would be $5,100. They needed $8,000. Thankfully, they had put so much away into their 401(k) and IRAs over the years that they were sure it would be easy enough to make up that difference each month.

But Michelle and Monty hadn't considered the fact that they needed not $8,000 gross but $8,000 *net* every month. This is because they had not taken into account taxes. Most of us think that when we retire our taxes will be lower, and we plan on that.

What we don't realize is that our 401(k)s come with a bargain with the IRS. We put the money into our retirement accounts *before* taxes, so in return, we pay taxes on the money we put in, *and* all the growth, when we take the money out in retirement! The IRS has patiently waited to collect their side of the bargain!

Michelle and Monty made sure to have the three legs of their stool in retirement, as they'd heard so many times. They knew that the third leg was their retirement accounts, but they didn't realize that at least 25% of that money didn't belong to them. It belonged to the IRS.

Michelle and Monty made three faulty assumptions that we see very often.

Assumption #1: They Won't Pay Much in Taxes, If Anything

It's a common myth that taxes will be significantly lower, even nonexistent, in retirement. If you remember from Chapter 6 about qualified money, retirement is actually the IRS's chance to collect on your retirement accounts that have been tax deferred until now.

Michelle's parents didn't pay taxes because they lived on Social Security alone. So, Michelle wrongfully assumed that she and Monty wouldn't have to, either.

Monty's parents had passed a long time ago and left him a large IRA, which became an Inherited IRA. There were taxes on the Inherited IRA, but it never occurred to Monty there might be taxes on their own IRAs. He had never talked about taxes with his parents. They always seemed to have enough income, so he hadn't given it much thought.

Assumption #2: There Will Be a Lot of Tax Breaks in Retirement

Michelle and Monty were devastated to learn that the only guaranteed tax break in retirement was an extra deduction of $1,350 each for a married couple who are both over 65 ($1,700 for a single person over 65). And they didn't know their Social Security would be taxed. Michelle's parents never paid taxes on Social Security because her parents' provisional income put them into such a low tax bracket, which we'll explain a little later.

With the income that Michelle and Monty needed, they would be taxed on 85% of their Social Security. Michelle's parents lived in one of the 37 U.S. states that don't tax Social Security. But Michelle and Monty didn't happen to live in one of these states.

Assumption #3: Net Income Is What Matters, Not Gross

Assumptions #1 and #2 led to assumption #3. Michelle and Monty assumed they just needed to fill the gap on expenses. They didn't consider how taxes might affect this. They calculated the net amount that they would need to take out of their IRA when they should have calculated the gross. The gross is the total amount from which taxes will be subtracted. The gross amount minus taxes equals the net amount they would actually get to spend per month.

So, the initial problem was that Michelle and Monty were sure they would pay fewer taxes in retirement. Because of this, they based their plans on net income, not gross. But what we dropped on them next was the real bombshell.

THE TAX BUCKETS OF RETIREMENT

All of Michelle and Monty's hard-earned money had been shifted into their largest asset outside of their home: their 401(k) and other retirement accounts. They never worked on developing other assets that were more tax-efficient. Because of this, their Social Security would be taxed even more. Tax-efficiency was the key ingredient they missed when making their plan.

Michelle and Monty wanted to know what they could have done differently. First of all, we told them, they could have diversified their investments. And by that, we didn't mean diversify among different securities or types of investments. Of course, we all should do that to prevent crashes in the market from killing our retirement, but what we meant was that Michelle and Monty should have diversified their investments among different "tax buckets."

Michelle and Monty had never heard of a "tax bucket." There are three tax buckets to consider in our savings for retirement.

Tax Bucket #1: Taxable Funds

In this first tax bucket are accounts like CDs that are taxed annually. You put money in the bank and you get a 1099 for interest at the end of the year, even if you didn't take the interest out. Later, if you want to take the money out, the taxes have already been paid.

Another example might be a brokerage account. You get a 1099 for capital gains every year. It would not be 100% taxable later when you liquidate the account. Only the remaining capital gains would be taxed, and then only at your capital gains rate based on your income.

Tax Bucket #2: Tax-Deferred Funds

The second tax bucket is the tax-deferred bucket. This is where Michelle and Monty had put all their savings. They didn't have to declare it as income when they contributed the money to the retirement accounts, so they didn't have to pay as much in taxes while they were working. It seemed to be a great bargain. They got a tax deduction, but it was a "bargain," as in an "agreement" with the IRS. We'll talk more about this later.

Tax Bucket #3: Tax-Free Funds

Last of all, there is the tax-free bucket. A Roth IRA, for example, would be in this bucket. These are after-tax IRAs that have no tax "bargain" with the government to pay taxes later. You pay the taxes when you contribute, and the contributions *plus* the growth are ***tax-free*** forever!

Keep in mind that things like Municipal Bonds interest is not income taxed, but it would add to "provisional income" to make your Social Security taxable. There is also life insurance, which we'll talk more about.

FILLING THE TAX-FREE BUCKET

Looking at their buckets, Michelle and Monty had about 5% in bucket #1, the taxable bucket; 95% of their money was in the tax-deferred bucket: 401(k)s, IRAs, and others. There was absolutely nothing in Michelle and Monty's tax-free bucket. And, again, Michelle and Monty wanted to know what they could have done differently.

I suggested that Monty could have contributed to his 401(k) as he did, but perhaps only up to the "match." Monty's employer was matching his contributions up to 3% of his salary, which would give him more money in his 401(k). Why would he *not* do it? A tax deduction and a match. Free money from his employer!

Yet if he'd stopped his own contribution at the matching amount, he may have also taken advantage of other options that would have been tax-free in the future. Of course, later in his career, he could have taken advantage of a newer plan that just had its 20th birthday—the Roth IRA or Roth 401(k), which became available in 2006.

Roth IRA and Roth 401(k)

The Roth IRA became available in 1997, well before there was a Roth 401(k). Monty possibly could have contributed to a Roth IRA any funds above his employer's match if he qualified. You can only contribute if your income is below a certain level, which has changed over the years, if you already have a 401(k).

The Roth IRA had contribution limits of $6,000/year in 2021 for people under age 50, and $7,000 for people over 50. However, if Monty didn't qualify because his income was too high, he may have been able to do a "backdoor" Roth IRA, which we'll come back to at the end of this chapter.

The Roth 401(k) became available in 2006. No income limit applies to contributions. For this type of account, Monty would have paid taxes on the money that was deferred into the Roth 401(k) from his salary. But Roth 401(k) contributions are never taxed in the future. Once the account is five years old, not even earnings are taxed.

Monty didn't realize this when his employer started offering a Roth 401(k). As they played catch-up after the kids were gone, Michelle and Monty could have been contributing to a Roth 401(k) through his employer. The contribution limit this year is $26,000 a year if you're over age 50 or $19,500 a year if you're under age 50.

Life Insurance

Michelle and Monty could also have put money into life insurance. This is a new one for a lot of people. Monty could have contributed up to his employer's match to his 401(k), then put all the extra money into a permanent life insurance policy. Monty didn't think he needed life insurance, but he did need an account that he could draw from and not pay taxes during retirement.

The trick is to purchase an indexed universal life policy with the lowest death benefit that allows the policy to accumulate cash value and still remain classified as "life insurance" (which gives it tax-advantaged rules). One reason for this, of course, is that in Monty's situation, he wasn't looking for a death benefit. The other is that a lower death benefit keeps the cost of insurance inside the policy down so the money can grow.

If Monty had put money into such an account, he could have contributed more money than necessary for the cost of the life insurance death benefit. This would have "over funded" the policy. In other words, he would have put in a lot of money that wouldn't go toward paying for death benefits but ***would*** grow without taxes.

Michelle and Monty would not have to pay taxes on the money as it grew. In fact, the indexed universal life cash value inside cannot go down with the market. But since the interest is tied to what the market does, and the "caps" and "participation rates" are much higher than fixed index annuities, it could grow dramatically.

In addition, Monty's 401(k) and IRAs, even his Roth IRA, all have penalties if he takes money out before age 59.5. But he could use the money inside the IUL policy at any age. When he and Michelle retired, they could have taken out loans from the account to live on. Loans are not taxable.

If you build up a large pot of money inside a life insurance policy, you can take income out as loans. As long as the policy has a "corridor" of life insurance, the loans are just subtracted from the death benefit. But *beware*, a mistake could make all the loans taxable!

Strategies like this are complex and require a specialized advisor to construct a policy that will work for you. Be sure to read the last chapter of the book to understand how to choose a competent advisor for your retirement.

But what about Michelle and Monty? Wasn't there anything they could still do? It seemed too late for the indexed universal life insurance. It was certainly too late to go back and do a Roth 401(k) or a Roth IRA. What could Michelle and Monty do?

GENERATING FUTURE TAX-FREE INCOME

But was it *really* too late for that indexed universal life? Actually, it wasn't. Michelle and Monty could use some of their 401(k), IRA, or other taxable retirement accounts to put money in an indexed universal life insurance policy if they wished. They could transfer some of that IRA money into an IRA annuity. They could then have the annuity pay a set amount toward an indexed universal life premium.

Michelle and Monty would still have to pay taxes on the money paid into the indexed universal life policy since it came out of their IRA. However, the money wouldn't be taxed all at one time, and it would set them up later for an income that was tax-free.

If they transferred the money to the life insurance policy all at once, they'd have to pay taxes on the large lump sum, which wouldn't be possible for them. Also, partial conversions of their IRA to a Roth IRA could be one step toward Michelle and Monty's plan for future tax-free income.

Converting Your IRA

What about the Roth 401(k) and Roth IRA? Well, you can't contribute to any IRA, not even a Roth IRA, once you are retired. Your tax return must show earned income during that year to contribute to it. Even if you can't contribute to a Roth IRA, you can convert an already existing IRA account into a Roth IRA account.

"My friend told me I can't convert anything to a Roth because I make too much money. I make over $100,000 a year," Monty said.

Actually, that law changed a few years back, and now Monty could convert to a Roth IRA, no matter his income. But if Monty converted all of his and Michelle's retirement money into a Roth IRA, it would cost them over $100,000 in taxes. They couldn't do that.

Michelle and Monty *could* plan to make conversions a little at a time, or do "partial conversions." How much should they convert to avoid a large tax bite? To determine this, they would have to "convert up to the bracket."

If you look at your tax return, there are tax brackets. Perhaps you're in the 22% bracket. If there's a difference between how much of your money is taxed at 22% and how much *could* be taxed at 22%, there's a gap between your income and the top of the bracket. You would want to convert just enough to stay in that bracket so that your income doesn't fall into the next higher tax bracket of 24%. This is what we explained to Michelle and Monty.

Michelle and Monty were 65. If they started right now, they could convert a good portion of their IRA to a Roth IRA before they turned 72 (because of the new SECURE Act there are no RMDs until age 72!). "But how will that help?" Monty wanted to know, "if we're going to be taxed on the money when we take it out anyway?"

Monty now fully understood his bargain with the government. He knew that he and Michelle owed the IRS taxes on their IRA every time they took money out for the rest of their lives. There are two reasons to consider converting, even though you pay taxes on the conversion. First, taxes are "on sale" until 2025—the lowest they've been in decades—and we don't know what the tax rates will be later. Second, you'll pay taxes on what you convert but *not* on the growth you take out later.

Monty thought tax rates would go up with the national debt. Then wouldn't you want to get your money out sooner, at the lowest possible tax rate? Monty agreed that he and Michelle did.

Michelle and Monty could begin converting with a plan in place. They could start with some money now and convert a little more every year until they turned 72. If they converted just $25,000 a year, they could have $175,000 tax-free by age 72, *plus* any growth would be tax-free as well. We explained that by doing partial conversions they would keep themselves in a lower tax bracket, reduce their RMDs, keep their Medicare premiums low, plus allow all this money to *grow* tax-free *forever*.

But why age 72? Because, if you remember from Chapter 5, at age 72 (instead of 70.5 as it was before the SECURE Act passed) the IRS will require that they begin taking money out of their IRA (RMDs). They will no longer be able to convert anything until *after* they take out what the IRS calculates each year as their RMD. "The government knows how long you will live," I told them.

Michelle laughed. "No, they don't."

We explained that the IRS tables say that now, at 72, they were going to live 25.6 more years. If they divide 25.6 into the value of their IRA on December 31 of the prior year, that will require them to remove 3.91% (almost 4%!) of their total value. That is the amount they will have to take out and pay taxes on.

For instance, if their total IRA or 401(k) value is $1 million, they'll have to take out $39,062.50 for the year and add it to their income for taxes. This is called a required minimum distribution, or RMD.

Every year, as you get older, the IRS factor used to calculate your RMD gets smaller, because they don't think you'll live as long. But because the "factor" is a divisor, the smaller the number, the higher the percentage you'll be taking out. It will be 6.76% a year by age 85, and the percentage keeps going up!

Michelle and Monty still weren't completely sold on the Roth IRA conversion plan. We explained that the money they converted to a Roth IRA would not only be tax-free but also RMD-free.

RMDs are only calculated on taxable money from your traditional IRA or 401(k). This meant that they would pay some taxes on the IRA, but by converting a good portion of those funds to a Roth IRA, they would set themselves up for tax-free growth and a tax-free future.

"Last question," said Monty. "Will my kids get the money tax-free if I do these conversions?"

"Absolutely," we answered. "With tax-free growth for up to ten years after they inherit it!" Prior to the passing of the SECURE Act, it would have been tax-free for the rest of their lives. Now most Inherited IRAs, if they're not left to your spouse, whether Roth IRA or not, have to be liquidated by the end of the tenth year. This only enhances the benefit of Roth conversions, because the Inherited IRA is 100% taxable in the tenth year after inheritance. (For more information, go to www.RetirePluggedIn.com/bookdownlads and download the SECURE Act white paper.)

Consider the SPIA

There were still other things that Michelle and Monty could do to lower taxes until they got to the tax-free money in their plan. They could reposition money from the CDs in the bank into another tool with a special regulation by the federal government. This tool is called a Single Premium Immediate Annuity, or SPIA. This is an annuity with a single premium, which we mentioned in the previous chapter.

Michelle and Monty could reposition some of their already-taxed money into a SPIA. It would be immediate income, and one with tax advantages according to the IRS exclusion ratio regulation (26 CFR § 1.72-4). The exclusion ratio excludes part of their income from taxes, while the rest of their income is taxed at ordinary tax rates. If Michelle and Monty paid an $85,000 premium, but will get $100,000 back over the next five years, they won't have to pay taxes on the $85,000 they put in, because it was already taxed. To find out how much of their income each month is taxed, we divide the premium ($85,000), by what they'll get back ($100,000) to get the "ratio." For Michelle and Monty, that "ratio" is an 80% return of their own money (premium), leaving only 20% of their income to be taxed.

Michelle and Monty could put together a plan for lower taxes now, while also planning to convert their IRA so they could move toward a tax-free income in the future.

Consider a Reverse Mortgage

Another possible tool in the box for Michelle and Monty was the reverse mortgage, as we also discussed previously. A reverse mortgage on their house would provide a tax-free income. I pointed out that they had no mortgage on their house. "I know," Michelle said, "and that's the way I want to keep it."

We all think we want our house paid off, but the question is, is this a tool you can use if you need income? A reverse mortgage may or may not be for you, but it will provide money. Just like when you bought the house and the bank gave you money to buy the house. With a reverse mortgage, they give you money, and because it's a loan, it's tax-free.

In fact, as mentioned before, you can split the reverse mortgage money up into three parts, if you wish. You can have an income every month guaranteed out of the value of your home, tax-free. You can have part of it as equity, as a lump sum that you can spend to upgrade your home or take vacations. You can have a portion that's just there for you to pull without taxes in case of emergency, or whenever you want it.

Michelle had heard the same kinds of myths about reverse mortgages as Paul and Shirley in the previous chapter. We explained that if Michelle and Monty were planning to stay in the house for the rest of their lives, their heirs would simply have to pay the mortgage back. No one would take the house. So that was another option.

But Michelle and Monty were still worried about their taxes. They were especially worried about being taxed on Social Security, which they had not expected. Michelle still didn't understand why her own parents weren't taxed on it, yet she and Monty would be. I said, "Okay, then. Let's look at why your mom wasn't taxed and why you will be unless we make a plan." A tax efficient plan was what they needed.

MAKING A TAX PLAN

The Social Security Administration figures out who should pay taxes on their Social Security income by calculating each recipient's Provisional Income. Your Provisional Income is calculated by adding half of your current Social Security income to *all* of your *taxable* income.

Taxable income in retirement includes your pension, your IRA or 401(k) withdrawals, your interest from CDs at the bank, capital gains on your investments, and the nontaxable interest from municipal bonds. Then they look at a chart like the one shown below (also included in Chapter 3) to decide how much in taxes you'll owe on your Social Security.

Social Security Taxable Portion

Provisional Income (AGI + Nontaxable Interest + ½ of Social Security Benefit) above the below amounts may result in a portion of social security benefits being taxable.

Single Filers	Joint Filers	Amount Taxable
Below $25,000	Below $32,000	0%
$25,000-$34,000	$32,000-$44,000	50%
Above $34,000	Above $44,000	85%

Social Security Taxable Portion Chart

Source: ssa.gov/benefits/retirement/planner/taxes.html

Michelle's parents weren't paying taxes because of their poor financial situation. They lived very frugally, with their only income being from Social Security. Only half of their Social Security counted toward provisional income. I asked Michelle, "According to this table, if you're married, at what break point does your Social Security become taxable?"

Michelle now understood why her parents did not pay taxes. She also saw that if she and Monty started taking money from their IRA, which is 100% taxable, they would bring themselves into the higher bracket. In this bracket, they would pay taxes on 85% of their Social Security.

And now, the tax-free bucket was starting to make more sense to them. They saw that if they moved IRA funds into the tax-free bucket, even though they had the income, it was tax-free. This meant it wouldn't show up on their tax return.

"That's our goal," Monty said. "If we don't show the money in our tax return, then our Social Security could be less taxable, or even tax-free."

Right now, Michelle and Monty were in a lower tax bracket because they were joint filers and married. They could have a lot more income still before they went into a higher tax bracket on their taxes, or before their Medicare premiums were raised because of higher income. This really gave them an opportunity to do those partial IRA conversions.

Unfortunately, if one of them passed away, the survivor would have to file single. Single tax rates are much higher, and provisional income breakpoints are a lot lower, meaning that the survivor will pay more taxes on less income.

Planning for a Survivor

We directed Michelle and Monty to look at the table below. According to the table, if a couple took out $20,000 a year from their IRA, they wouldn't pay much more in taxes. But if one person died, that would mean one less Social Security check. This often means the survivor has to take more from the IRA to continue to live the same. This means more taxable income right when that person is filing single at higher tax rates!

It's easy to see from the table below that taxable Social Security is less when you're married than taxable Social Security if you're single. In this particular example, the couple was paying $0 in taxes with a $40,000 Social Security income and $20,000 IRA income. But when one of them died, the survivor had to pay over $5,000 in taxes on the same $60,000 income.

2021	Single/Widow $40,000 IRA $20,000 SS Social Security	Married/Joint $20,000 IRA $40,000 SS Social Security
Taxable Social Security	$17,000	$4,000
Taxable Other income (IRA)	$40,000	$20,000
Total Taxable Income	$57,000	$24,000
Minus Standard Deduction	-$14,250	-$27,800
Net Taxable Income	$42,750	$0
Total Federal Income Tax	$5,153.28	$0

Chart of Taxable Social Security and IRA for Single Versus Joint Income

This is where the planning comes in. They have to plan so that if one of them passes, the other one will not have these tax penalties. They must have some tax-free income to avoid it. And it only gets worse from here!

If Michelle had to take out an additional $10,000 to afford to pay the taxes, that would raise her taxes also! The year your spouse dies, even if it's January 1, you can file joint. But the next year, you're considered "single" for tax purposes whether you're a widow/widower or not. Compare the tax tables for 2022 for a single income versus a joint income below.

Tax Rate	For Single Filers	For Married Individuals Filing Joint Returns	For Heads of Households
10%	$0 to $10,275	$0 to $20,550	$0 to $14,650
12%	$10,275 to $41,775	$20,550 to $83,550	$14,650 to $55,900
22%	$41,775 to $89,075	$83,550 to $178,150	$55,900 to $89,050
24%	$89,075 to $170,050	$178,150 to $340,100	$89,050 to $170,050
32%	$170,050 to $215,950	$340,100 to $431,900	$170,050 to $215,950
35%	$215,950 to $539,900	$431,900 to $647,850	$215,950 to $539,900
37%	$539,900 or more	$647,850 or more	$539,900 or more
Source: Internal Revenue Service			

2022 Tax Brackets for Single Filers, Married Couples Filing Jointly, and Heads of Households

Source: https://taxfoundation.org/2022-tax-brackets/#brackets

If you are married filing joint, you don't go into the 24% tax bracket until your joint income exceeds $178,150 + your $25,900 automatic deduction + your $2,800 deductions if you're both over age 65. That means you can have an income up to $206,850 and still be in the 22% bracket!

But if you're single, you go into the 24% tax bracket when your income exceeds $89,075 + your $12,950 automatic deduction + your $1,750 deduction if you're over 65. With an income over $103,775, now you're in the 24% tax bracket!

Michelle didn't think this was fair. "I would still have to pay 100% of the mortgage, and my utility bill wouldn't be cut in half."

We then showed Michelle how Medicare premiums are calculated. Again, looking at a table for single versus joint taxable income, we saw that those who are alone are penalized. The premiums are based on modified adjusted gross income (MAGI) reported on your tax return. Tax-free income is *not* reported, which could substantially change the calculation. The table below illustrates the great disparity for a widow/widower.

If your yearly income in 2020 (for what you pay in 2022) was			You pay each month (in 2022)
File individual tax return	File joint tax return	File married & separate tax return	
$91,000 or less	$182,000 or less	$91,000 or less	$170.10
above $91,000 up to $114,000	above $182,000 up to $228,000	Not applicable	$238.10
above $114,000 up to $142,000	above $228,000 up to $284,000	Not applicable	$340.20
above $142,000 up to $170,000	above $284,000 up to $340,000	Not applicable	$442.30
above $170,000 and less than $500,000	above $340,000 and less than $750,000	above $91,000 and less than $409,000	$544.30
$500,000 or above	$750,000 or above	$409,000 or above	$578.30

Medicare Part B Premium for Single Versus Joint Income

Source: https://www.medicare.gov/your-medicare-costs/part-b-costs

If a married couple has an income at or below $182,000, their premiums are only the basic $170.10/month. While your spouse is alive, you can have $150,000/year income and pay only $170.10/month each! However, if a widow or widower can maintain that $150,000/year income, the premiums would jump up to $442.30/month! And those premiums are net of taxes. Your annual cost just for Medicare Part B goes from $2,041.20/year to a whopping $5,307.60/year!

If the widow has to take out more IRA money to maintain her life-style, and this puts her in the 24% tax bracket (not to mention state taxes of an average 5%), she would need to take a gross amount out of more than $6,000 additional just to pay her Medicare premiums! How fast would her IRA reserves be liquidated with all these additional taxes and withdrawals?

DEATH AND TAXES

Unfortunately, Michelle and Monty's story is all too common. They thought they'd done everything right. It was lucky for them that they decided to seek out an independent retirement planner, just in case. Planning for taxes is essential. You may not be able to escape death, but you can find ways to mitigate taxes.

Tax efficiency is what will secure your future. A tax-efficient retirement plan can raise your net income and lower your taxes. It provides security against outliving your money because Uncle Sam took a big bite out of your hard-earned savings. As we discussed in this chapter, there are plenty of tools you or an advisor can use to put a tax-efficient plan in place. You can convert your tax-deferred IRA money into a tax-free Roth IRA. You can consider a reverse mortgage or a SPIA. Life insurance can be another option.

The key to tax-efficient planning is to make sure that you don't have all your money in the taxable or tax-deferred bucket. You need some assets in the tax-free bucket too. Provisional income may even be something that can work to your advantage. You can go to www.RetirePluggedIn.com/bookdownloads to see how provisional income may affect your retirement.

We also have a free white paper for you at www.RetirePluggedIn.com/bookdownloads on the "backdoor" Roth IRA we mentioned earlier in this chapter.

In the next chapter, we look at what we can do to protect our independence and also protect our families from losing our hard-earned assets. Estate planning is certainly about leaving a legacy for your children or heirs, but even more importantly, it's about putting together the proper paperwork to protect you during incapacity and end-of-life decisions; this is done with Powers of Attorney, Living Wills, Trusts, and other essential documents.

9

ESTATE PLANNING AND LEGAL DOCUMENTS

Do You Have the Power?

Do you have the power to take care of everything that might happen in your retirement? Carmen and Keith thought they did.

After years of worry, Carmen had finally dragged Keith in to plan with us. Keith had assured her they were prepared—until they faced that transition from saving and investing to living on his pension, Social Security, and their 401(k). Keith realized he really didn't know how to put the whole thing together. So, we helped them make a Life Income–Living Asset Cycle℠ plan.

Carmen said that Keith refused to face problems until they "hit him upside the head." Keith laughed, "I'm so glad we've got the plan together, but she's right. I'd rather look at what's going right than what could go wrong." Carmen and Keith were ignoring the final component of retirement planning—**Decision #9: How do I plan for incapacitation and passing on my assets?**

We were soon to learn that there were other very serious things going on in Carmen and Keith's lives. Things that could go very wrong if they didn't adequately prepare for them. Keith's parents were making serious decisions without considering consequences. His parents didn't seem to be able to handle their affairs anymore, and Keith worried it was soon going to be his responsibility. In fact, when he last visited, he'd found they had been scammed out of money.

"They seem to be giving money away to anybody who calls," Keith said. "Bills are going unpaid. And we've got our financial plan together now, but I'm worried about Mom and Dad."

Carmen's family wasn't doing much better. Her mom had passed away. Her dad had remarried, but now his new wife had passed away. Carmen's dad still had quite a bit of money. In addition to Carmen and her brother, Carmen's father had three stepchildren. But he had no plan of how to take care of himself or what would happen if he passed. It would likely all fall on Carmen's shoulders.

Carmen and Keith didn't know how to handle these problems. Would they have the power to be able to help their parents and take care of everything? Keith said, "I'm looking at my parents, and I'm looking at Carmen's dad, and I'm wondering, what about us? I mean, what happens if we get to this point? Who's going to help us? How do we make sure that things don't go wrong?"

Beside their parents, Keith and Carmen had a daughter they were worried about. They considered her husband greedy and were worried he might get his hands on the inheritance they were hoping to leave her. They also had a grandson on Social Security disability benefits. They'd heard that if they left money to him, he might lose his benefits. It turned out that Keith and Carmen had a lot more to plan for than they initially realized.

INTRODUCTION TO ESTATE PLANNING AND LEGAL DOCUMENTS

"These are all valid concerns," we told Keith and Carmen. "And they can all be solved with estate planning, and the right legal documents drawn up and tailored to your particular situation."

Keith thought this all sounded scary. Estate planning was for the rich—people who have millions of dollars. Like many of us, Keith and Carmen had heard about rich people avoiding estate taxes. They'd heard about rich people getting Trusts and other legal-sounding documents that would be too complicated (and expensive), they thought, for them.

But for most of us, estate planning is not about estate taxes right now. That's because most of us don't have $12.06 million in assets to worry about. Yes, the federal estate exclusion amount for 2022 is $12.06 million *per person*, and it goes up each year with inflation thanks to the 2017 Tax Cuts and Jobs Act. Of course, this is just until a new Congress and president change it, or it "sunsets" in 2025 and reverts to the pre-2018 exemption level of $5 million per taxpayer.

"Estate planning is for when you die," Carmen said. "I'm worried about now. And anyway, we already have a Will. And I think my parents have a Will too."

What Carmen didn't know is that if we pass away, or our parents pass away, a Will requires that the assets go into Probate. We'll go into more detail about Probate later in the chapter, but in short: Probate is the thief of your legacy and the fate of all estates without a good estate plan!

In addition, proper estate planning is also "life planning." Hopefully, most of us are more concerned about taking care of our parents while they're alive; good estate planning takes life circumstances into account as well.

Patti and I are not lawyers. We don't give legal advice. But as a Certified Estate Planners (CEPs®), we could help Keith and Carmen coordinate with a lawyer to make sure all their goals would be accomplished if there was any incapacity. Lawyers prepare documents, but we interpret or translate the legalese that can be so confusing.

There were still some important legal forms that Carmen and Keith needed to learn about.

HIPAA Waiver

We asked Carmen what seemed like an obvious question: "If Keith had an accident while he was out alone, and he was brought to the hospital, unconscious, would the hospital call you to let you know?"

"Of course."

"If Keith is unconscious, he can't sign a legal document called a HIPAA Waiver. If he can't sign the waiver, the hospital will not call you."

The unintended consequence of the HIPAA law is that now, by law, the hospital cannot notify a relative if the patient has not signed this waiver. They cannot even tell you, if you call the hospital, whether a family member is there. They can only tell you if the family member is conscious and has already signed the waiver.

In fact, there was a woman in our area whose husband got into this situation. He left for work one morning but he never arrived home. His wife called his coworkers, and they said he was fine when he left work. She called the nearby hospitals and they all said, "I'm sorry, ma'am. We cannot tell you if that gentleman is here or not." She couldn't find him.

The woman's husband actually died in one of the hospitals she called. They were not allowed, by law, to tell the woman that her husband was there. A simple piece of paper called the HIPAA Waiver would have allowed her to get the information. Carmen could have told the hospital she had a HIPAA Waiver signed by Keith and would provide it for them, so they could have released his information. This is why the HIPAA Waiver is one of those documents that everyone needs.

But this isn't the only essential document. There are more.

Financial Power of Attorney

"Keith, you have that large IRA rolled over from your 401(k) that we invested for you, right? But imagine something's happened to you and you can't function, and Carmen needs it to pay bills. How does she get at the money in that IRA?"

"Oh, that's no problem," Keith said. "She's the beneficiary on it."

Unfortunately, a beneficiary cannot touch the money in the account unless the holder on the account has passed away. We told Keith about one of our clients, Betty.

Betty's husband had gotten dementia. He had a quarter of a million dollars in an IRA, and she needed that money for his care. Betty was the beneficiary, but she could not touch that money. We were eventually able to get Betty the money, but not without a fight.

Betty had a legal, valid, Financial Power of Attorney that would allow her to act on all is financial accounts just as if she were him. It was drawn up by a lawyer and signed by Betty's husband, but there is no law that forces an institution to accept a Power of Attorney, even when it's legal, valid, and signed. Why would they refuse it, you might ask? Well, a Power of Attorney could be given to Betty today, then given to someone else tomorrow.

How does the institution know there isn't another Power of Attorney out there? What if they accepted it, and they were sued by someone who held another Power of Attorney over her husband? The institution wanted her to use their form to avoid this. The problem was, of course, that her husband couldn't sign it.

We were finally able to submit the Power of Attorney form that she had had for years. Submitting this form allowed her to sign his name on their Power of Attorney form so that she could get the money.

This is an example of how an advisor can help you, of course. But most importantly, this story shows the kinds of complications any of us could run into without a specific signed form for Financial Power of Attorney. Without that original form, Betty would have been stuck.

Other Powers of Attorney

A Power of Attorney is necessary to access your parents' bills and help pay them. If you don't have a Durable General Power of Attorney (a Power of Attorney that allows the Power of Attorney to handle almost any financial matter, not just a specific one, and stays valid until revoked), you would have to get guardianship of your parents. In fact, if something happened to Keith, and Carmen didn't have a Durable General Power of Attorney, she would have to get guardianship of her own husband in order to handle his affairs. She would have to go to court and pay thousands of dollars. It would take months to get that piece of paper so that she could touch the money in his IRA.

And what about medical decisions? We asked Keith if he'd looked at his parents' medical records. He hadn't. Of course, even as their son, he wouldn't have access to that information. But worse yet, without a Medical Power of Attorney, Keith couldn't make decisions for his parents if they were unable to make them. Unless everyone in the family is in complete agreement, a doctor will not act without a signed piece of paper that says you have the right to make those decisions.

"How do I decide whether they should have, you know, life support? Can I make those decisions?"

With a Medical Power of Attorney, Keith could make these decisions for his parents. Carmen could also make these decisions for her dad.

A Living Will

A Living Will is important to have for end-of-life care issues. It is unrelated to your "Will," which directs your assets at death. It's important to discuss these issues with your parents and make sure they have a Living Will so you'll have direction as to what they want when the time comes. It's just as important to discuss these issues with your children and make one for yourself so they're not left guessing what you want, and therefore guessing what they should do.

We believe a Living Will should have three options:

Put me on life support.

Don't put me on life support.

Put me on life support but take me off if it isn't helping.

You can get a special Living Will that is valid in 42 states and the District of Columbia called the "Five Wishes." It gives all three options listed above. The "standard" state version of most "Living Wills" only gives two options:

Put me on life support. (Your family may not be able to get you removed, even though you're in a vegetative state and all your assets are being liquidated.)

> **Don't put me on life support.** (Most people don't want to be kept on life support if they are brain dead or in a vegetative state, but almost everyone wants a chance.)

A great example of why we may need life support temporarily is Nora's mother's case. My mom developed congestive heart failure after a lifelong habit of smoking. This caused fluid to build up around her heart, making it impossible for her to breathe. She would be brought to the hospital, seemingly near death's door. The EMT would insert a breathing tube, then the doctors would draw off the fluid, and in 24–48 hours she'd be fine.

This happened three times, and it extended my mother's life, with great quality of life, for over 15 years! She didn't want to be kept on life support indefinitely, but she sure didn't want to die prematurely. When she was almost 90, she decided she didn't want to have any life support. She said she had lived a good life, and her quality of life was declining, so she changed her wishes.

Keith and Carmen agreed that they needed a good Living Will for their parents and for themselves. A Living Will is an estate planning document usually included as part of an "ancillary package" that should be included in your estate planning documents.

"What about the Will we already have?" Carmen asked. "That should work if we die, right?"

This brings us back around to the subject of Probate.

PASSING ON YOUR LEGACY

Wills and Probate Court

A Will demands Probate. Probate means going to court and collecting what the deceased has left to you. Carmen understood this much of it. Yet she hadn't really thought about all that might entail. Probate is the legal process of proving a last will and testament, verifying that the will is legal and deceased person's intentions are carried out. The deceased's property must be identified, inventoried, and appraised (including everything in their house). "Lawyers are expensive. Oh, I don't even want to think about going to court."

In most states, it takes a year to two and a half years to settle Probate before you can get the assets. Probate is also public, meaning anybody can go to court and read about everything that you own and who's getting what. You may not care about publicity, but would you want scammers, for example, to know exactly what your child will inherit? Carmen and Keith did not want that.

For many of us, a Will is the only way we think we can pass on our legacy. But there are actually three common ways most people pass on their assets: Joint Tenants with Rights of Survivorship (JTWROS), contractual beneficiaries, and Probate.

Joint Tenants with Rights of Survivorship (JTWROS)

If you own a house together, you are "joint tenants." JTWROS is the type of ownership typically used with your spouse. If one owner passes, the survivor now owns the property—no Probate! The survivor doesn't even have to go to court to claim the property. Ownership simply passes automatically.

This is often used not just by spouses but also for a widow or widower to pass ownership to a grown child or other family member. But problems can arise from using this method of passing your home on to family members other than a spouse. The reason for this is that ownership doesn't just happen when you pass. With JTWROS, it is effective immediately!

Thus, if you add a family member to your house JTWROS and that family member suddenly gets a divorce, now your house is a part of the assets being divided in their divorce. If you add a child JTWROS and someone decides to sue them, now your house is their asset in the lawsuit, too.

Remember that JTWROS is ownership. And it is effective immediately.

Let's look at Grace's situation. Grace was widowed when her girls, Rose and Marlene, were only two and four years old, respectively. Grace fought her way through life, raised the girls, and became successful in her career. Eventually, Marlene married and moved across the country. This meant that, as Grace got older, she would have to rely mostly on Rose, who still lived nearby. Rose never married and gladly took on the responsibility.

Grace added Rose to everything JTWROS, including her home, so Rose could handle her assets if she were incapacitated. Rose would then split the assets with Marlene when Mom was gone. Grace had bought her home for $200,000 back when the girls were little. It was valued at $600,000 when Grace passed away and ownership passed on to Rose through JTWROS.

One of the benefits of the tax law is something called "step-up in basis." When you pass away, whatever you own has a "step-up" from the original basis (the amount you paid for the asset) to the value on your date of death. Instead of having to pay capital gains tax on the difference between what you paid for it and what it sells for now, the heirs pay no taxes if it sells for the value on your date of death.

Grace had bought her home for $200,000, but she didn't own the home alone when she passed. When she added Rose to the deed, it gave Rose half of the original $200,000 basis, or $100,000. Rose was JTWROS, so Mom's half of the $600,000 home value got a step-up in basis, from $100,000 to $300,000 (half of the value on Grace's date of death). But since Rose didn't die, her half did not get a step-up in basis to $300,000.

Could that be a problem? Let's look at the chart below.

Tax Problems: JTWROS Home Inheritance Purchase Price: $200,000 Value at Death: $600,000		
Mom's Half		**Rose's Half**
Value at Death	$300,000	$300,000
Minus Basis	-$300,000 (stepped-up at death from $100,000)	-$100,000 (No step-up because Rose didn't die!)
15% Capital Gains Taxable	$0.00	$200,000
Cap Gains Owed	$0.00	$30,000

Rose would never cheat her sister, but she now faced a dilemma: how do I give Marlene half and not cheat *myself*? When Rose sold the home for $600,000, she owed capital gains taxes on $200,000, or a minimum of $30,000 in taxes! Does she give her sister *less* than $300,000, half the home's value? How does she explain that to Marlene? Or does she pay the taxes and take the loss herself?

In addition, the law says that you can only give away $15,000/year without reporting the gift to the IRS on Form 709. Rose has half the house to give her sister and half the $150,000 bank account and all the other assets she was JTWROS on as well!

Did Grace want to cause problems for her girls? Of course not! Could she have added *both* girls to the assets? Yes, but that wouldn't have solved the problem. They would still lose part of their inheritance to unnecessary taxes. As well, Grace was fortunate that Rose was never sued or married and then divorced.

We'll look at a much better solution to this issue later in this chapter.

Contractual Beneficiaries

A second way to pass on assets is by contract. That is, assets with a built in "contractual beneficiary." Contractual Beneficiaries are available in life insurance, annuities, 401(k)s, TSPs, IRAs, and other retirement accounts. If Carmen is designated the beneficiary on Keith's IRA, then when he dies, it goes directly to her without having to go to court. When you have a beneficiary on any asset, it goes directly to the beneficiary without going through Probate or even a Trust.

But first of all, not all assets can have a contractual beneficiary. Most states don't allow a beneficiary on a real estate deed, or on a vehicle title. Brokerage accounts that are not retirement accounts don't automatically have the ability to add a beneficiary, and some bank and credit union accounts do not allow it. Some states and institutions do allow it, but then we have to look at the second problem.

Second, if you can put a beneficiary on the asset, it doesn't solve your problems if you're incapacitated. Carmen, as beneficiary, becomes the owner and gets control only when Keith dies. If Keith is incapacitated, and they have no other planning, Carmen would have to go to court to get "guardianship" of Keith to handle his assets. We call that "Living Probate." That can be as bad as Probate at death. It can be a lengthy, costly, and a humiliating process for Keith.

Last, you'd think writing beneficiaries would be easy. Just name them! Carmen and Keith would name each other first, or "primary." Then their children, Karen and Kyle, would be named next, or "contingent." Their daughter, Karen, has two children, a boy and a girl; Kyle has three very young boys. So, what happens if Karen predeceases Carmen and Keith? Or if Kyle predeceases them? Would Carmen's children get her share? Would Keith's children get his share?

There are two ways to write beneficiary designations: "per stirpes" or "per capita." "Per stirpes" behind Kyle's name would mean his children would get it if he predeceased receiving his share. If that isn't written on the form, the default for almost all beneficiary forms is "per capita," which means the other beneficiary named (Kyle's sister, Karen) would get it *all*, and Kyle's children would be accidentally disinherited, probably right when they needed it because their dad is gone!

Carmen said, "Didn't you say a Trust would solve all this for the kids? And for us?"

A Trust

Keith was convinced that a Trust sounded too complicated. He knew that it was ANOTHER legal document. Why make it even more complicated than a Will? But we reminded him and Carmen about Probate. Everything goes to Probate when people die, whether you have a Will or not.

Probate has a purpose. People have no problem taking the assets of the deceased, but nobody wants to pay the bills. So, it's mandatory, by law, that if someone dies, their assets have to go to Probate so the court can figure out what bills need to be paid before the beneficiaries get the assets. That's the purpose behind it.

"What does a Trust have to do with that?" asked Keith.

A Revocable Living Trust is just like an invisible box during your lifetime. You're creating a legal document and giving your assets the name of that legal document, rather than your name. Think of it like you're creating an invisible box to put all of your assets into. You put them in the box by "re-titling" those assets with the name of your document, the Trust. You'll die someday, but that invisible box doesn't. That means there's no Probate!

Keith said, "Wait! I won't *own* my assets?"

There are three people involved in the Trust:

1. The **Trustor**: The person putting the assets into the Trust. That's *you*!
2. The **Trustee**: The person controlling the assets. That's also *you*!
3. The **Beneficiary**: The person who benefits from the assets. During your lifetime, that's *you*!

In other words, *you* are the Trust, and the Trust is *you*, because the Trust is invisible during your lifetime. And since the box is invisible, during your lifetime, no one sees it. Everything stays in your name, you just put the word "Trustee" behind your name. Your checking account stays the same. Everything stays the same. Only when you die does that box become visible. But it's still not public.

Let's look at the process:

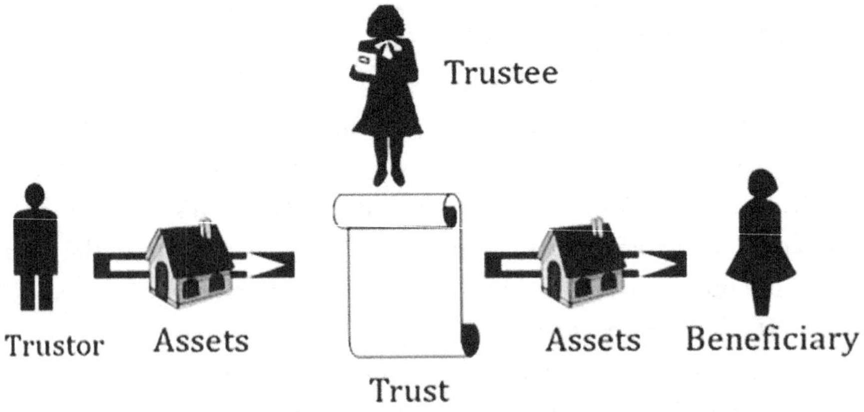

The Process of Creating a Trust

The Trustor (you) puts your assets into the Trust. The Trustee (you) handles the assets for the benefit of the beneficiary (you) during your lifetime.

If you become incapacitated or die, since nothing goes to court, the Trust is handled by the Successor Trustee you have named. The Successor Trustee acts as you and handles all your assets for your benefit. This might be your child, a friend, or a company you name if you have no one to do it. The Successor Trustee looks in the box and says, "Oh, the instructions in here say sell the house and split the money between the children. Give my necklace to my granddaughter, and give my gun to my son." The Successor Trustee does what you say. No lawyers involved. Just hand out the assets.

However, you cannot escape your debts, even with a Trust! Your Successor Trustee has a fiduciary duty to pay your bills before distributing your assets. A fiduciary is bound both legally and ethically to pay your debts and follow your wishes stated in the Trust, no matter what they think is best. The difference between Probate and a Trust is that there is no public information on your assets with a Trust, eliminating the false claims that often happen during Probate. And no court to hold your assets hostage!

If you're considering a Trust, you should know that estate planning for living and for death does cost. A Will is fairly inexpensive. A Trust is about three to four times the cost of a Will. However, if you go through Probate with a Will, the cost will be much more than the cost of the Trust. In Probate, in addition to the fees paid to the lawyer and the executor, there may also be appraisal fees, court filing fees, bond fees, legal fees, and accountant fees. You can probably count on your estate paying anywhere from 4% to 7%, of the assets for Probate, plus the fees mentioned above! (Source: https://www.thebalance.com/how-much-does-probate-cost-3505268.)

Let's look at an example. If you own a home valued at $500,000 and have bank or investment accounts of $100,000, we're talking anywhere from $30,000 to $90,000 to get through Probate. The average Revocable Living Trust may cost $3,500–$5,500, maybe a bit more, depending on your state, your lawyer, and how complex you want to make it.

The question is, when do you want to pay? Lawyers have a saying: "Pay me now or pay me later." If you pay now, you pay less. If you pay later, you pay much more!

It was Carmen and Keith's choice, but a Trust could definitely help keep that greedy son-in-law from taking their daughter's money, and it could make sure that their disabled grandson got what he needed (because, with a Trust, that box could hold the grandson's money so that he didn't lose his government benefits). The daughter's money could be held in a Trust only for her benefit, outside her husband's reach. With estate planning, we could help solve these problems for Keith and Carmen.

Keith and Carmen held hands. They looked at each other. They smiled. They said, "I guess this is the final piece. Let's get this done."

ESTABLISHING A TRUST

The first step for anyone who wants to establish a Trust is always to figure out what you want to accomplish. Anyone can create that box. If you go to a lawyer, he or she will write a document called a Trust. But is it the right kind of Trust for you?

There are three basic kinds of Trusts and many variations of each.

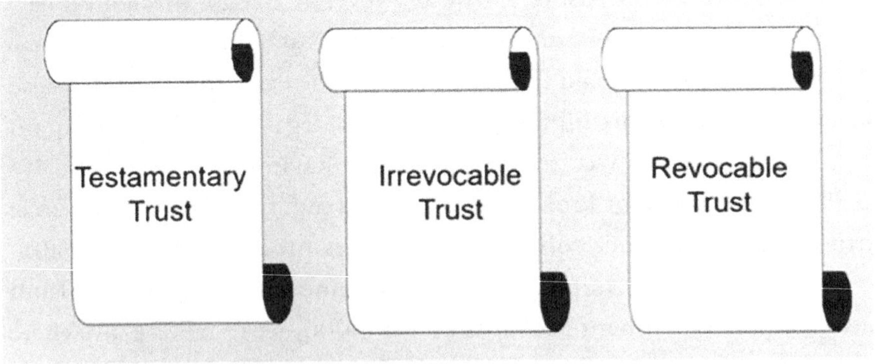

Types of Trusts

Carmen's Aunt Bea had a Trust, but everything still went to Probate when she died. It took almost two years to divide everything up. Carmen told us that was one of the reasons she had been so hesitant about a Trust at first.

Testamentary Trust

Carmen's aunt had a "Testamentary Trust." What this means is that the lawyer had written a Will for Aunt Bea, not a Trust! If a Trust doesn't exist before you die, the Will makes everything go through Probate, then the executor creates the Trust with the assets left, under the supervision of the court, which costs a lot more money.

If the lawyer had written a Will and a Trust, there would have been two documents at Aunt Bea's passing. If her assets were titled into the Trust (renamed in the name of the Trust), there would have been nothing to go through Probate, and it would have been settled quickly and easily.

There could be many reasons for a lawyer to write a Testamentary Trust. Maybe he didn't understand what Aunt Bea really wanted, or maybe he was trying to keep her costs down now, figuring her estate could pay later. Or maybe he saw an easy way to make more money later.

There is a lawyer joke in which one lawyer asks the other, "Do you have a retirement plan?" The other answers, "You bet! Do you know how many Wills I have in my drawer?" Most people are overwhelmed at the thought of Probate and courts, so they go back to the lawyer who drew up the original Will. They then pay a lot of money for the lawyer to take it through Probate.

Irrevocable Trust

Keith then shared about his uncle who went into a nursing home. His family said they didn't have to pay for it because he had a Trust. Could Keith and Carmen's Trust hide their assets so the government would pay through Medicaid, like with his uncle?

Not with the type of Trust we've been discussing, a Revocable Living Trust. A Revocable Living Trust is "invisible" during your lifetime, but you control the assets and get the benefit of the assets, so you're not poor enough to qualify for Medicaid.

Keith's uncle probably had the second type of Trust, called an Irrevocable Trust. This type of Trust is exactly what it says, irrevocable. Once it's done, you can't change your mind. You have to give your assets to the Trustee of that Trust, who can not be you. Most people wouldn't consider an Irrevocable Trust unless they're facing near-death issues.

"So, what *is* a good fit?" asked Carmen.

That would be determined by your assets, your goals, and what you want to accomplish. Unless your lawyer knows your purpose of getting a Trust, what your assets are, and how you want things distributed, he or she won't know what type of Trust would be best for you. This is why we recommend that you find certified estate planning professionals like us.

Revocable Living Trust

To establish a Revocable Living Trust, a Certified Estate Planner (CEP®) works with you to interpret what you need to prepare for the lawyer. They will assist you in getting the proper documents from the lawyer by providing the key information that determines what type of Trust the lawyer needs to create and the family issues that need to be addressed. Most families use a Revocable Living Trust because it can be changed during their lifetime, unlike an Irrevocable Trust. Also, it avoids Probate completely, unlike a Testamentary Trust.

If you have property out of state, or other property besides your home, then you're going to want to put all of those things in that "invisible box." A local lawyer cannot prepare deeds in another state, but a good CEP® will be able to connect you to lawyers in those states who can do it for you.

With property, such as your home, the lawyer will simply make a new deed with both of your names as Trustees of your Living Trust. That puts your house in the Trust. And if you have a house you inherited from a relative in another state, a lawyer in that state can put that property into your Trust as well. As long as you title it and put it into that box through a deed, you will not have any Probate in any state. That property immediately goes to whomever you say.

So, the first step is to work with a CEP® who will work with a lawyer to write a Revocable Living Trust tailored to your personal needs. Then a certified estate planning professional will help you put everything into the Trust by assisting you in changing the title on your accounts to say "Your name, Trustee."

You can put your furnishings and personal effects into the Trust with a simple document that comes with the Trust: all of your knickknacks, your clothes, your gold in the basement. Everything is put into the Trust without you having to make a list or get an appraisal.

Once your Revocable Living Trust has been set up legally, every "thing" that you own is in the Trust without having to take an inventory. What many people don't know is that if you go to Probate court, your heirs have to list every fork, knife, spoon, lamp, piece of furniture, and item of clothing in your house, not to mention all the tools in the garage. They then have to assign a price or an appraised value to it and bring it to the courthouse for approval. That list becomes public information, so anyone can check to see what's in your house. What a nightmare!

But with this Revocable Living Trust set up by a lawyer with the assistance of an estate planning professional, everything is in that "invisible box." No long inventory list is required. Once the Trust is established with the legal documents, and we've titled everything into the Trust, the Trust is funded. Now, it is as simple as having your Successor Trustee, perhaps your child, pay your final bills and distribute everything when you're gone.

This is the benefit of a Revocable Living Trust. Your assets can quickly and easily be passed on without being tied up in Probate. This avoids costing everyone time and money. The process of setting up a Trust also ensures that you have your important documents in order, like a HIPAA Waiver for your spouse, as well as Financial Power of Attorney and a Living Will, If you want to know more about what documents you should have in a good estate plan, you can go to the RetirePluggedIn.com/book-downloads site.

We have mentioned again and again the importance of finding the proper advisor for your journey into retirement—someone who knows how to decumulate and effectively navigate the changing tax laws. Now is the moment you've been waiting for. In the next part of this book, we'll walk you through the process of finding an independent fiduciary advisor to help advise you with your retirement plan, and we'll discuss the decision to plan your retirement yourself.

NINE RETIREMENT DECISIONS: WITH OR WITHOUT AN ADVISOR

Everything in this book should come together to open the door to freedom. We want you to enjoy your retirement knowing everything is in place. Let's look at one final case study to see how this might work. Jason and Theresa dreamed, they planned, and they accomplished everything—from completely remodeling their home to establishing their own business. They did everything themselves.

When Jason's parents retired, Jason was the one who researched and found the answers for them. Any personal assistance they needed, Theresa was there to help. No one questioned Jason and Theresa's ability to speak for Jason's parents, or anything like that. Everything went smoothly. When Jason's parents passed on, all assets had been jointly owned with the children so nothing went to court. Things were a bit more complicated with Theresa's mother, but overall, they'd handled both of their parents' situations well.

Now that Jason and Theresa were planning to retire, it seemed there were more laws now to be addressed. And Jason and Theresa saw their friends' parents, and even some of their own friends, have big problems in retirement with taxes and health care. Nobody had anticipated these problems. They always thought they could do it all themselves, but it was becoming pretty scary to think about managing their own retirement. What if they made a mistake?

With some digging, Jason and Theresa could find reliable information about specific topics on the internet, but sources conflicted about how to put it all together. Medicare, Social Security, IRAs versus Roth IRAs, 401(k)s, pensions. It was all there, but how should they best put it all together into a plan that worked?

In addition to their internet research, Jason and Theresa went to seminars about retirement. It seemed the speakers just wanted to sell them their services. From investment advisors to insurance advisors, estate planning attorneys, and CPAs—every time Jason and Theresa talked to a professional, they looked at things only through their lens of expertise. And since no one was selling Medicare or Social Security, no one at the seminars would talk about these things. And, like on the internet, there was a lot of conflicting information.

Jason and Theresa didn't know who they should believe. They wanted to talk to someone who knew everything about retirement, not just about whatever aspect they were selling. CPAs told them how to save money on their taxes today but not how to plan for taxes during their retirement. Insurance "professionals" advised Jason not to take a survivor benefit on his pension. They said, "No, no, no. It's better for you to buy life insurance." They called it "pension max."

Theresa trusted Jason's knowledge about investments, but his parents had it quite easy when they retired, and there were no problems when they passed on. But Theresa's mom lived a lot longer than her father. She was a widow, living all alone. Things became really tough.

Theresa said, "You know, Jason, all this long-term care I've given my mother? Well, I know there's long-term care insurance, but some people say you shouldn't buy it. How do we know the right thing to do? Can we really do this ourselves?"

Jason felt a huge weight of responsibility to take care of Theresa and make it easy for her and the kids if he were gone. He began to think they might need to find someone who could help them put all the pieces together so that they could both rest easy.

It wasn't just life insurance or annuities or long-term care insurance. It wasn't just their tax returns or putting together legal documents. They needed someone who would work with them to coordinate all the necessary professionals and all their goals into a plan tailored to their future—a plan based on what they were trying to accomplish and what was going on in their lives.

Jason and Theresa had always had the philosophy that you do the best you can at something, and then you fix it if it goes wrong. Jason understood the value of learning from his mistakes, but there were no do-overs in retirement.

So, on the advice of a friend, Jason went to see a number of Certified Financial Planners, or CFPs. But everyone he interviewed wanted to talk about investing his money. Jason was already good at investments. It was all the other aspects of retirement they needed help with. Jason and Theresa needed an overall advisor who would listen to their goals, look out for them, and help them put a comprehensive plan together. But where would they find this person?

TRUE FIDUCIARY, OR FIDUCIARY ADVISOR

Finally, Jason learned that the person they were looking for is called a Certified Financial Fiduciary (CFF®). A true fiduciary, by law, has to put their interests behind yours. At this time, no firm by law is a fiduciary. Only advisors holding certain investment licenses are required to put their client's interests before their own.

Currently, the only rule that insurance agents are held to is the "suitability" rule. Something that is "suitable" for a 65-year-old doesn't mean it's the right tool for that particular client.

Many investment advisors, who are fiduciaries, don't have the insurance licenses or estate planning background to assist in all areas of retirement. One important caution: if an advisor is not "dual licensed," meaning insurance and investments, they're not capable of creating a plan based solely on your needs not theirs. A true fiduciary advisor who can put your interests first will not be limited in their field of expertise by having only an investment license. That way they can see all the possibilities and opportunities to make a retirement plan work.

We believe a competent advisor for retirement must be "agnostic to the tool." In other words, they don't care what the product is, or what company it's from. They only care that it meets the needs of their client. If an advisor ever says to you that "*all* investments are too risky" for retirement, or "*all* annuities are *bad*," *run the other way!* There is good and bad in *every* investment or product. The question is, does the good outweigh the bad, and does this investment or insurance product fulfill the needs of *your* retirement?

A CFF® must meet rigorous requirements, pass background checks, pass an exam, and keep up with the latest rules and laws about being a fiduciary. If Jason and Theresa narrowed their search to a fiduciary advisor, particularly a CFF® who is "dual licensed," they could find someone who would listen to them. They could probably even find someone highly experienced, with hundreds of clients who have retired and had their problems solved successfully.

CAPTIVE ADVISORS

Most of the people Jason had been talking to were captive advisors. A captive advisor works exclusively for one company. What that means is they can only do business with that company. They can't go out into the universe of solutions and find the right ones for you. They have to use the tools given to them by their company.

A company's priority is normally to develop business within the company, not to send a client someplace else. This means that a company can force a captive advisor to discontinue doing something that might be in the client's best interest if it is not also in the company's best interests. It is the parent company, not the client, that is a captive advisor's first priority. By contrast, an independent advisor can represent a lot of different companies.

Recognizing a Captive Advisor

To recognize a captive advisor, first look for the firm's name. Is it an insurance company or an investment firm that has a multitude of advisors? If these advisors belong to a large firm, they are not independent. They are not able to do whatever they want.

This is counterintuitive for most of us. We think, "I don't want that little one-shop guy down the street because he doesn't have backup." But most of the large firms have captivity in some way or another. In reality, an independent advisor actually has the backup of all the large firms that they work with. They can pick and choose what might work best for you from a multitude of large companies rather than being locked into the services of one.

One of the major mistakes that Jason found himself making at first was avoiding independent advisors because they didn't have the backing of a big name he recognized. The bigger the name, the more likely the advisor is captive.

INDEPENDENT ADVISORS

Because independent advisors represent many different companies, they can look at different investments and present more opportunities to their clients. An independent advisor has the freedom to find an answer anywhere. An independent advisor also has the ability to compare prices and products, features and services, and find that one that will best work for you. This was exactly what Jason and Theresa wanted.

Finding an Independent Advisor

So now Jason knew that he and Theresa were looking for an independent advisor who is a fiduciary. He wanted a person who was very knowledgeable about retirement issues, and he found that some advisors actually taught educational classes rather than giving a sales pitch. Advisors have to be able to explain what they do very well in order to do this. Jason started looking for advisors who gave educational seminars at a library or webinars online, for instance, or who taught a college adult education class.

But Jason also needed an IRA specialist. He knew a lot about investing to accumulate his retirement money, but not much about decumulation. He knew even less about protecting his money in retirement.

Jason quickly learned that finding a fiduciary in the insurance and annuity world was not easy. First, he wanted someone who had been vetted as a CFF®. Second, he wanted someone who was verified to have knowledge about safe investments.

Finding the right kind of advisor can be even more difficult when you don't know where to look. This is why we have compiled a list of sites we consider trustworthy for research help.

RECOMMENDED SITES LISTING ADVISORS WITH CREDENTIALS

Knowing your potential advisor's credentials is necessary for comprehensive retirement advice. We've all heard about many designations, such as CFP, but those initials don't mean they're knowledgeable and experienced in retirement planning! The sites described below will help you find an advisor who has been background-checked and specializes in retirement planning.

https://brokercheck.finra.org/ The official site for FINRA (Financial Industry Regulatory Authority). Use this site to check an advisor's background. A broker is not the same as an investment advisor or a Registered Investment Advisory Firm. Enter an individual's name or a firm name to see how long they were registered as a broker, and whether there are any disclosures you would need to know about. If you see a "PR," it means they were previously registered as a broker (commission-based representative). If there is an "IA," it means they are currently a fee-based fiduciary. Click on "Visit SEC Site" to see their current status.

https://www.adviserinfo.sec.gov/ The official site for the Securities and Exchange Commission (SEC). Use this site to check out an investment advisor or Registered Investment Advisor. Choose either "Individual" to search for a person, or "Firm" to search for a firm. Click on "Get Details" to see if there are any "Disclosures" showing criminal history, investigations, disputes, or the like.

https://www.irahelp.com/ The official site for Ed Slott and Company, LLC, America's IRA Experts. Click on "Elite" and choose "Find an Advisor" from the dropdown. A "Master Elite" is the most highly qualified to answer questions about the proper handling of retirement accounts and the rules, laws, and changes that apply to them. These advisors take three-day educational classes every six months, and an exam twice a year.

http://nationalcffassociation.org The official site of the National Association of Certified Financial Fiduciaries (NACFF®). Search the Certified Financial Fiduciary (CFF®) Directory for member advisors. These advisors have successfully completed a rigorous certification and training process established by NACFF® and agree to uphold the highest moral, ethical, and fiduciary standards of service when providing investment advice to potential and existing clients.

https://nicep.org/ The National Institute of Certified Estate Planners (NICEP) website. Click on "Find a Professional" to find a currently accredited CEP®. A CEP® has completed a rigorous eight-module course of instruction in the field of estate planning, successfully passed a comprehensive proctored examination process, shown a desire to associate with professional estate planning peers, agreed to comply with annual estate planning continuing education requirements, and ascribed to the practical guidelines and code of ethics of NICEP.

https://www.ethics.net/ The National Ethics Association (NEA) website. This organization checks for accuracy and authenticity of members and provides ethics courses, ongoing education, and certification of members. To find a member, scroll to the very bottom of the page and click on "Member Directory." To verify a member, scroll to the bottom of the page and click "Verify a Member." NEA is devoted to aiding consumers in the increasingly complex task of conducting due diligence on business professionals. This results in greater peace of mind for skeptical consumers and rewards those worthy of their trust.

https://www.ltc-cltc.com/ The Certification for Long-Term Care (CLTC®) website. Click on "Find a CLTC®" at the top of the page. Search for someone who has been a CLTC® for at least ten years, so they can guide you through all the changes that have occurred. This site lists professionals who have taken courses on long-term care, not just insurance, and how to fund long-term care from many different sources.

https://safemoney.com/ SafeMoney's tagline is "Retirement Made Safe." The site features independent annuity and life insurance product information for the public. Insurance professionals licensed and trained in annuities and life insurance are listed on the site. Click on the "Advice" tab and choose "Locate a Licensed Advisor." Financial professionals featured on SafeMoney.com develop personalized retirement plans that preserve wealth, offering guaranteed incomes that are tax advantaged and earn interest without being subject to costly market downturns.

http://chfebc.com/ The official Chartered Federal employee Benefits Consultant℠ site. If you are a federal employee, look for a Chartered Federal Employee Benefit Consultant℠ (ChFEBC℠). These advisors are educated and tested on federal employee benefits. Their education is updated annually and tested for competency. Click on any state on the map to locate a ChFEBC℠ in your area or enter an advisor name in the Search box to check if they are qualified.

If you are fortunate enough to locate an advisor who is listed on five or more of these sites, you have a good candidate! If you can find someone listed on *all* of these sites, you've hit the jackpot!

ABOUT RETIREPLUGGEDIN.COM

Many do-it-yourselfers can do their own planning if they have the resources and guidance they need. Jason figured he could do a lot of it himself, especially when he discovered the www.RetirePluggedIn.com membership site. Not only did the membership site provide accurate and up-to-date information, but it also offered a step-by-step, how-to approach to all the issues he might encounter in retirement, and how to coordinate them. For every retirement question he had, it was easy to find the rules and how they might apply to his situation (with instructional videos and illustrations). Maybe he didn't need an advisor after all!

All of Jason and Theresa's personal and financial information could be entered to create a step-by-step program using the unique Life Income–Living Asset Cycle℠ system offered on the site. One concern Jason and Theresa had was how they could be sure their estate plan would be available to their loved ones if they needed help. Their estate planning documents could be placed in a digital vault, with chosen "deputies" to be given access in case of an emergency.

The membership site provided not just information and step-by-step planning tools but alert messages triggered to be sent according to Jason's personal plan. Jason would be notified through www.RetirePluggedIn.com when he reached an age of eligibility, when an enrollment window opened, or when a deadline was approaching.

Jason could retire "unplugged" from the worries of keeping track of eligibility dates, deadlines, actions required for tax efficiency, and making sure to avoid penalties, because his retirement is "plugged in" to the answers he needs. He would have alerts sent to remind him that he could now roll over part or all of his 401(k), for example, with a link to the website education giving explanations of why he would or would not want to do that.

Plus, Jason would get information on *when* he should access his Social Security statement with a link to how to download it, how to read it and *check for accuracy*, and what to do if it's *not* accurate. Based on his age, he'd be alerted *when* to apply for Social Security and Medicare, with a link to education on the website explaining his options, deadlines, and penalties if he didn't take the proper actions. He was relieved to know these would keep him on schedule no matter what he was doing, or where he was going.

However, sometime after Jason became a member of the RetirePluggedIn.com site, he thought, "You know, I did find that one advisor who I really liked. I might work with him." What he soon learned was that www.RetirePluggedIn.com gave him the information he needed to understand what the advisor was saying. It alerted him when to get in touch with the advisor to get things done. Although he really didn't need an advisor for his plan any longer, he felt it might give Theresa some comfort to have someone to talk to if he predeceased her. It's not uncommon that one spouse truly understands the challenges and can do it themself, and the other spouse may need someone to turn to if alone.

When Jason decided he would like an annuity as part of his guaranteed income, he found he would need an advisor to access that tool. When he decided tactical management was what he wanted for part of his portfolio, he needed to find an advisor who has access to such managers. Jason learned that for some things it made sense to get help. And with www.RetirePluggedIn.com he could "trust but verify." This was the right tool for him and Theresa.

Jason really liked that every month he received reminders. In January, he was reminded to look for 1099s for his taxes, with explanations of when to expect them based on whether they were coming from employment, a bank, or an investment firm. He didn't know that investment firms are not required to send out their 1099s until the end of February. He filed his taxes one year, then had to go back and amend on his return!

Even better, with the link in the email, he went directly to the website education on 1099s and was able to know for sure how to read them so he could check for errors and get them corrected if necessary—*before* filing! The deadlines for filing changed yearly, extensions too, but he received timely notifications early so he could prepare. Again, with links in the email to the education on the website as to who can get an extension and how to get it. He especially liked that the information was not only in video format but also audio and transcript. All this, and it was just January!

Every month of the year, the information came directly to Jason's inbox. No wondering, no searching, no missing deadlines. Social Security announced whether there would be a cost-of-living increase in October, and Jason received notice of it and how it was calculated. Every time there was a change in tax rates for the coming year, Jason was notified with a link to the new tax tables on the website and explanations of how it would affect tax returns.

We've heard so many times that knowledge is power, but first, it has to be accurate, up-to-date knowledge. Second, we need to know how to apply it.

In summary, these are the nine retirement decisions we *must* make:

Decision #1: How will I fund my needs after the day I retire?

Decision #2: Do I have a lump sum or income for retirement?

Decision #3: How and when do I claim my Social Security?

Decision #4: How do I prepare for a long-term care need?

Decision #5: How do I use my qualified money most tax-efficiently?

Decision #6: How should I invest during retirement?

Decision #7: How much guaranteed income do I need, and how do I get it?

Decision #8: How do I use my savings tax-efficiently to increase net income?

Decision #9: How do I plan for incapacitation and passing on my assets?

The www.RetirePluggedIn.com website can help provide both kinds of knowledge. What we're hoping to do through this book and the membership site is what Jason ultimately accomplished. We want to hand you the keys to unplug from worry and be able to live retirement on *your* terms. We want to give you Peace of Mind and a Successful Retirement by plugging you in to the answers you'll need no matter how the rules change! You can do it!

NOTES FROM NORA AND PATTI TO OUR BELOVED READERS AND CLIENTS

Thank you *so much* for reading our book and working with us! For those of you we're meeting for the first time through our book, let us explain *why* the book and the website are so important to us!

We educate those looking at retirement, and those already in retirement, through workshops at libraries and universities, as well as webinars online on a regular basis. Many of those who attend ask for our help because, before they had the education, they had no idea how complicated it is to retire worry-free and successfully in the United States today!

Unfortunately, many come to us to "fix" an issue that was caused by lack of knowledge on their part, or on the part of an advisor they had been working with. The rules for all the issues we face in retirement, from income planning to Social Security, Medicare, IRAs, pensions, estate planning, and tax efficiency only get *more* complicated every year!

The government continually adds rules and changes rules, but never seems to take any rules away! Patti and I spend hundreds of hours and tens of thousands of dollars attending conferences, studying rule changes, taking exams, and applying the knowledge to retirees' situations every year. We've learned that far too few advisors care enough to do that. We've also learned that we have a finite amount of time to serve new clients, no matter how much we'd like to help everyone.

This brings us to why we have felt compelled to write this book and create the www.RetirePluggedIn.com membership site. Both Patti and I suffered significant personal problems and financial losses at the hands of an advisor long before we became advisors. We discuss these in the introduction.

We may never know if they intentionally misled us to make money, or if they were unaware of how what they did would affect us because of lack of knowledge. But I like to give the analogy of being poisoned because there was arsenic in your cup of coffee. Does it matter whether the arsenic was dropped in accidentally or intentionally put there? No. You are dead either way!

The only way for us to help more people avoid disastrous consequences in retirement is through up-to-date education. Between this book and our RetirePluggedIn.com membership site, we provide the tools you need to know what is in your own best interests based on the constantly changing retirement rules. We sincerely hope this provides you with all the tools you need to have a comfortable, "unplugged," and successful retirement!

GLOSSARY

Term	Meaning
401(a)	A retirement plan generally offered by government and nonprofit employers, similar to the 401(k)s offered by private employers.
401(k)	A defined-contribution retirement plan that allows employees to elect salary deferrals excluded from the employee's taxable income (except for designated Roth deferrals), which may have matching employer contributions.
403(b)	A retirement plan offered to employees of certain tax-exempt or not-for-profit organizations (like schools, certain educational institutions, or hospitals).
457	A type of nonqualified, tax-advantaged deferred-compensation retirement plan available for governmental and certain nongovernmental employees.
ADL	Activities of Daily Living: bathing, continence, dressing, eating, toileting, and transferring.

Advanced Medical Directive	*See* Living Will.
Annuity	A tax-deferred account with an insurance company. An annuity can be used for accumulation and/or income, as opposed to an "annuitization," which is a lump sum of money given in exchange for a guaranteed income stream.
Beneficiary	Any person who gains an advantage or profits from something. Typically refers to someone eligible to receive distributions from a Trust, Will, or insurance policy.
Capital Gains Tax	Capital gains are the profits you make when you sell a stock, real estate or other taxable asset that increased in value while you owned it. The capital gains tax is based on that profit. The long-term capital gains tax rate is typically 0%, 15% or 20%, depending on your tax bracket. You do not have to pay capital gains tax until you've sold your investment.
CD	A Certificate of Deposit, generally offered by banks, is a low-risk (often low-return) savings tool earning interest in a relatively safe way.
CEP®	Certified Estate Planner™: a financial, legal, or tax professional who has earned certification through the National Institute of Certified Estate Planners (NICEP).

CFF®	Certified Financial Fiduciary: a professional designation for financial professionals who have successfully completed a rigorous certification and training process established by the National Association of Certified Financial Fiduciaries, have undergone a background check, and agreed to uphold the highest moral, ethical, and fiduciary standards of service.
CFP	Certified Financial Planner™: a designation bestowed by the Certified Financial Planner Board of Standards. It is not specialized but includes a variety of areas in managing finances with a fiduciary requirement.
CLTC®	Certification in Long-Term Care is a designation recognized and supported by The American College of Financial Services and the National Association of Insurance and Financial Advisors (NAIFA). A CLTC® has acquired the critical tools necessary to discuss the subject of longevity and its acute consequences on a client's family financially, physically, and emotionally and provides advice that leads to a plan to mitigate those consequences.
Contractual Beneficiaries	Persons or entities named as the beneficiary of a contract, such as a life insurance policy, annuity, CD, and so on. Such beneficiaries receive the proceeds directly, rather than through Probate.
CPA	A Certified Public Accountant acts as a consultant on issues such as taxes and accounting.

Decumulation	The de-accumulation of assets in order to maintain your quality of life in retirement, which requires more planning than the accumulation of assets for retirement. Decumulation involves setting up lifetime income sources, positioning and tax-efficiently drawing down taxable, tax-deferred (401[k], IRA, etc.) and tax-exempt (Roth) assets while managing RMDs (required minimum distributions) against marginal tax rates.
Dollar-Cost Averaging (DCA)	An investment strategy in which an investor divides up the total amount to be invested across periodic purchases of a target asset to reduce the impact of volatility on the overall purchase, without regard to the asset's price, and at regular intervals. Automatic monthly contributions to a 401(k), IRA, and the like would be an example of DCA.
Durable General Power of Attorney	A Power of Attorney legal document that both authorizes someone to act in a wide range of legal and business matters and remains in effect even if the person is incapacitated. *See also* Power of Attorney.
Earnings Test Exempt Amount	The amount you can earn without losing Social Security benefits if you take Social Security below Full Retirement Age (FRA), also known as Normal Retirement Age (NRA). If you earn more than the specified amount for that year ($19,650 in 2022), you lose $1 of benefits for every $2 you earn over the Earnings Test Exempt Amount.
Exclusion Ratio	An exclusion ratio is established by IRS 26 CFR § 1.72-4. This ratio excludes part of an annuity income stream from taxes, while the rest of the income is taxed at ordinary tax rates.

FDIC	Federal Deposit Insurance Corporation: an independent agency created by Congress to maintain stability and public confidence in the nation's financial system. It insures bank deposits, limited to $250,000 per depositor, per bank.
FICA	The Federal Insurance Contributions Act requires a payroll tax of 7.65% be deducted from salaries to contribute 6.2% to Social Security and 1.45% to Medicare. The Employer is required to match this for a total of 15.3% FICA.
Fiduciary	A fiduciary must put your best interest above their own. A financial advisor who is a fiduciary has an ethical duty to recommend the best investments for you.
Financial Power of Attorney	Refer to entry for Durable General Power of Attorney for definition.
FINRA	Financial Industry Regulatory Authority. An independent nongovernmental organization that writes and enforces the rules governing registered brokers and broker-dealer firms in the United States.
FRA	Full Retirement Age, also known as Normal Retirement Age (NRA), as defined by Social Security, is 66 if you were born between 1943 and 1954. FRA increases incrementally if you were born from 1955 to 1960 until it reaches age 67.
Guaranteed Income	An income stream guaranteed to continue for a specified time or lifetime, no matter market or account value.

Head of Household	Taxpayers may file tax returns as Heads of Household (HOH) if they pay more than half the cost of supporting and housing a qualifying person. Taxpayers eligible to classify as HOH get higher standard deductions and lower tax rates than taxpayers who file single or married filing separately.
HECM	Home Equity Conversion Mortgage, often called a "reverse mortgage," allows one who is at least age 62 to borrow part of their home equity with no payments until they die or leave their home.
HIPAA	Health Insurance Portability and Accountability Act of 1996. This act was passed to ensure the confidentiality, integrity, and availability of medical information. To release medical information, one must sign a "HIPAA Waiver."
HIPAA Waiver	A legal document releasing doctors from the Health Insurance Portability and Accountability Act, allowing them to provide information on a patient's health to third parties, such as family members and other doctors.
Investment Advisor	Financial professionals who make investment recommendations or conduct security analysis in exchange for a fee. Investment advisors, also known as "financial advisors," are required to uphold standards of fiduciary responsibility.
IRA	An Individual Retirement Account allows you to save money for retirement in a tax-advantaged way. The account must be set up with a financial institution as the "custodian."

IRMAA	The Medicare Income Related Monthly Adjustment Amount is an amount you may pay in addition to your Part B or Part D premium if your income is above a certain level, for which the Social Security Administration (SSA) sets four income brackets that determine your (or you and your spouse's) IRMAA.
Irrevocable Trust	A type of trust whose terms cannot be modified, amended, or terminated without the permission of the named beneficiary or beneficiaries (*not* the original person who set it up!).
IRS	The Internal Revenue Service is the revenue service for the United States federal government, which is responsible for collecting taxes and administering the Internal Revenue Code, the main body of the federal statutory tax law.
IUL	Indexed Universal Life Insurance allows the owner to allocate cash value amounts to either a fixed account or an equity index account. It offers tax-deferred cash accumulation for retirement while maintaining a death benefit.
JTWROS	Joint Tenants with Rights of Survivorship is a type of account owned by at least two people who have an equal right to the account's assets and are afforded survivorship rights in the event of death of another account holder.
Large Cap Stocks	Refers to a company with a market capitalization value of more than $10 billion. Large cap is a shortened version of the term "large market capitalization."

Living Trust	Also known as a "Revocable Living Trust," a Living Trust is created during an individual's lifetime. A designated person, the Trustee, is given responsibility for managing that individual's assets for the benefit of the beneficiary(ies).
Living Will	A written statement detailing a person's desires regarding their medical treatment in circumstances in which they are no longer able to express informed consent. Also called an Advanced Medical Directive.
Medicaid	A public health insurance program that provides healthcare coverage to low-income families and individuals.
Medical Power of Attorney	A legal document that appoints someone as your representative and gives that person the power to act on your behalf for medical decisions in case you become incapacitated because of medical reasons.
Medicare	The federal health insurance program for people who are 65 or older, and certain younger people with disabilities or End-Stage Renal Disease.
Medigap	A Medicare Supplement Insurance that helps fill "gaps" in Original Medicare and is sold by private companies.
Municipal Bonds/ Interest	A municipal bond, commonly known as a muni, is a bond issued by state or local governments, or entities they create such as authorities or special districts. Interest income received by holders is often, but not always, exempt from federal and state income taxation.

Mutual Fund	A company that pools money from many investors and invests the money in securities such as stocks, bonds, and short-term debt.
PIA	The "primary insurance amount" is the benefit (before rounding down to next lower whole dollar) a person would receive if they elect to begin receiving Social Security retirement benefits at their normal retirement age, also known as "Full Retirement Age." At this age the benefit is neither reduced for early retirement nor increased for delayed retirement.
Power of Attorney (various kinds)	A legal document that gives authority to act for another person in specified (financial, legal, medical) or all matters.
Predecease	To die before another person, typically someone related by blood or marriage (as in "His wife predeceased him.").
Probate	Probate Court is a segment of the judicial system that primarily handles such matters as wills, estates, conservatorships, and guardianships as well as the commitment of mentally ill persons to institutions designed to help them.
Prohibited Transaction	Any improper use of your IRA by you, your beneficiary, or a disqualified person, which includes your fiduciary and members of your family including spouse, lineal ascendants, and lineal descendants and their spouses.

Provisional Income	The IRS threshold above which Social Security income is taxable. It comprises one half of Social Security benefits plus all other taxable income AND interest on Municipal Bonds.
Qualified Money	Refers to money in retirement accounts, such as IRAs, 401(k)s, and 403(b)s, on which you do not have to pay taxes on the gains until you start withdrawing the money.
Reverse Mortgage	Also called a "Home Equity Conversion Mortgage" or HECM, it allows one who is at least age 62 to borrow part of their home equity with no payments until they die or leave their home.
Reversionary Annuity	A Reversionary Annuity is a retirement income strategy that combines an insurance policy with an immediate annuity for a surviving spouse. The beneficiary receives a guaranteed lifetime income instead of a lump sum payment when the insured party dies.
Revocable Living Trust	A Trust whereby provisions can be altered or canceled by the Grantor(s) or originator(s) of the Trust during their lifetime(s), and the estate will be transferred to the beneficiaries upon the Trustor's (Grantor's) death, bypassing Probate Court.
RMD	A "required minimum distribution" is the amount of money that must be withdrawn from an employer-sponsored retirement plan, Traditional IRA, SEP, or SIMPLE annually, beginning at age 70.5 prior to 2020, changed to age 72 in 2020.

Rollover — An IRA Rollover is a transfer of funds from a retirement account into a Traditional IRA or Roth IRA either by direct transfer or by a check, which the custodian of the distributing account writes to either the new custodian or the account holder who then must deposit into another IRA account within 60 days.

Roth 401(k) — An employer-sponsored investment savings account that is funded with after-tax dollars up to the plan's contribution limit.

Roth IRA — An individual retirement account that offers tax-free growth and tax-free withdrawals in retirement as long as you've owned your account for 5 years and you're age 59.5.

SEC — The U.S. Securities and Exchange Commission is an independent federal government regulatory agency responsible for protecting investors, maintaining orderly functioning of the securities markets, and facilitating capital formation.

SEP — Simplified Employee Pension (SEP) plans provide business owners with a simplified method to contribute toward their employees' retirement as well as their own retirement savings. Contributions are made to an Individual Retirement Account (IRA) set up for each plan participant (a SEP-IRA).

SIMPLE — "Savings Incentive Match Plan for Employees" (SIMPLE-IRA). Employers can choose to make a non-elective contribution of 2% of the employee's salary or a dollar-for-dollar matching contribution of the employee's contributions to the plan up to 3% of their salary.

SMA	A Separately Managed Account is a portfolio of assets managed by a professional investment firm with a wrap fee of 1%–3% per year of assets under management.
Social Security	The term used for the Old-Age, Survivors, and Disability Insurance (OASDI) program in the United States, run by the Social Security Administration (SSA), a federal agency.
SPIA	A "Single Premium Immediate Annuity" is a contract in which you pay an insurance company a lump sum of money up front, known as a premium, in exchange for guaranteed payments for life or over a set period of time. It can begin paying out immediately after purchase or within the year.
Successor Trustee	The person responsible for administering the Trust after its Grantor (Trustor/originator) either passes away or becomes "incapacitated"—that is, unable to administer the Trust for themselves.
Tactical Management	Tactical management looks at the present and the near future and attempts to shift the composition of a portfolio to manage risk exposure or to take advantage of new opportunities. This is a hands-on style of investment management.
Tax-Free	Refers to certain types of goods and financial securities (such as municipal bonds) that are not taxed. It also refers to earnings that are not taxed. Tax-free may also be known as tax-exempt.

Testamentary Trust	A provision in a Will that appoints a Trustee to manage the assets of the deceased. This trust is established after the estate has gone through Probate Court.
TRICARE	The health-care program for U.S. uniformed service members, retirees, and their families, which provides comprehensive coverage to all beneficiaries including health plans, special programs, and prescriptions.
Trust	A fiduciary relationship in which one party, known as the Trustor, gives another party, the Trustee, the right to hold title to property or assets for the benefit of a third party. Often used to refer to just one kind of trust, a Revocable Living Trust **in which the Trustor, Trustee and Beneficiary are all the same person.**
Trustee	A person or firm that holds and administers property or assets for the benefit of a third party.
Trustor	An individual who gifts funds or assets into a Trust by transferring his or her fiduciary duty to a third-party Trustee, or themselves as Trustee(s) during their lifetime(s), who maintains the assets for the benefit of the beneficiaries.
TSP	The Thrift Savings Plan is a retirement plan for U.S. civil service employees and retirees as well as for members of the uniformed services. It closely resembles a 401(k) plan.
VA	U.S. Department of Veterans Affairs
Will	Sometimes called a "last will and testament," a document that states your final wishes. It is read by a county Probate Court after death, which makes sure your final wishes are carried out.

Made in the USA
Monee, IL
04 November 2026

67387179R00095